THE MYSTERIES OF ALMSGIVING

A Translation from the Arabic with Notes of the

Kitab Asrar al-Zakah

of

Al-Ghazzali's ***Ihya' 'Ulum al-Din***

by

NABHI AMIN FARIS

KITAB BHAVAN
New Delhi-110002

Kitab Bhavan
Publishers, Distributers, Exporters & Importers
1784, Kalan Mahal, Darya Ganj
New Delhi-110002 (India)

Phone : (91-11)23277392/93, 23274686
website : www.kitabbhavan.com
e-mail : nasri@vsnl.com

2nd Edition : 2008

ISBN : 81-7151-161-9

Published in India by:
Nusrat Ali Nasri for Kitab Bhavan
1784, Kalan Mahal, Darya Ganj
New Delhi-110002 (India)

Printed in India at:
H.S. Printers
New Delhi-110002

CONTENTS

CONTENTS

PREFACE

Though one of the most important works coming down to us from medieval Islam, no single part of the *Ihya' Ulum al-Din* appeared in English, or any European language at that, until Duncan B. Macdonald published in the *Journal of the Royal Asiatic Society* (1901, pp. 195-252, 705-748, and 1902, pp. 1-28) an English version of Book VIII of the second quarter of the *Ihya'* , i.e. the *Kitab Adab al-Sama' w-al-Wajd* (On Audition and Grief). The second complete part of the *Ihya'* was Edwin E. Calverley's translation of Book IV of the first quarter, i.e. the *Kitab al-Salah* (Madras, 1925). Except for a few extracts and selections, no complete translation of any part of the *Ihya'* appeared in English until 1962 when two books from it were finally published: Book I of the first quarter, namely the *Kitab al-'Ilm* (The Book of Knowledge) translated by the present writer and published by M. Ashraf, Lahore; and Book III of the fourth quarter, namely the *Kitab al-Khawf w-al-Raja'* (On Fear and Hope), translated by William McKane and published by Brill of Leiden. The following year, 1963, saw also the publication, in English, of two other books of the *Ihya':* Book X of the second quarter, on the Conduct of Life as Exemplified by the Prophet (*Adab al-Ma'ishah wa-Akhlaq al-Nubuwah*), translated by L. Zolondek and published also by Brill; and Book II of the first quarter, i.e. the *Kitab Qawa'id al-'Aqa'id* (The Foundations of the Articles of Faith), translated by the present writer and published also by Ashraf.

The following pages present in English garb Book V of the first quarter, namely the *Kitab Asrar al-Zakah* (On the Mysteries of Almsgiving). The translation is based on three printed texts and one in manuscript form. The printed text are: first, that printed at Kafr al-Zaghari in A.H. 1352 from the older Cairo edition of A.H. 1289; second, that contained in the text of the *Ithaf al-Sadah al-Muttaqin bi-Sharh Ihya' 'Ulum al-Din* of al-Sayyid al-Murtada al-Zabidi (d. 1791); third, that reproduced in the margin of the same *Ithaf al-Sadah;* and fourth, the text preserved in a four-volume manuscript in the Garrett Collection of Arabic Manuscripts in the Princeton University (No. 1481). In the translation of Qur'anic verses, I have depended mainly on J.M. Rodwell's version.

It is my hope that by makind still another Book of the *Ihya'* available in English, non-Arabic-speaking scholars will draw a benefit, even from my mistakes.

Nabih Amin Faris

March 29, 1966

On the Mysteries of Almsgiving

INTRODUCTION

In the name of Allah the Merciful, the Compassionate. [190] Praise be to Allah who hath blessed some with happiness, and reduced others to destitution; who hath brought some to death, and others to life; who hath caused some to laugh, and others to weep; who hath brought some things into existence, and other things He brought to nought; who hath reduced some to poverty, and hath made others rich ; who hath visited some with harm, and others He hath blessed with good things; who hath created life from emitted clot,[1] and then set Himself apart from His creation through His attribute of independence (*ghina*) and endued some of His servants with excellence, enriching with His blessings those who toil and labour, and withholding His rewards from those who are indolent and languid, for the sake of testing them and trying them; who hath made almsgiving (*zakah*) one of the foundations of religion; and hath revealed that, by His grace, through the giving of alms are His servants justified and through the same is their wealth increased. May the peace of Allah be upon Muhammad the elect, the Lord of creation and the sun of guidance, and upon his family and his Companions who are favored with learning and piety.

To proceed we say: Allah has made almsgiving one of the pillars of Islam placing it next to prayer which is the supreme [duty in Islam]. Thus He said, "Observe prayer

1. Cf. *Surah* LIII: 43-50

and pay alms."[2] The Apostle said, "Islam was built on five [pillars]: to witness that there is no god but Allah and that Muhammad is His servant and Apostle, observing prayer, giving alms, [performing the pilgrimage, and fasting Ramadan]."[3] Furthermore, Allah has strongly warned those who are remiss in the fulfilment of these duties. Thus he said, "To those who treasure up gold and silver and expend it not in the way of Allah, announce tidings of a grievous torment."[4] "To expend in the way of Allah" means to set aside the right proportion [of one's wealth] for alms. Al-Ahnaf ibn-Qays said, "I was once in the company of a group of Qurashites when Abu-Dharr passed by a said, 'To those who treasure wealth announce that they will be branded in their back with a red-hot iron rod which will penetrate through their chests, and in the back of their heads with a rod which will pierce through to their foreheads.' " According to another version, the red-hot iron rod will be placed on the nipples of their breasts and forced through to emerge from the centre of their shoulder-blades, and on the centre of their shoulder-blades to emerge from the nipples of their breasts.

Abu-Dharr said, "I came upon the Apostle of Allah sitting in the shadow of the Ka'bah, and when he saw me he said, 'Verily they [191] are the lost ones; by the Lord of the Ka'bah, they are the lost ones.' I asked, 'Who are the lost ones? He replied, 'Those who have the most of wealth except him who gives of it to his fellowmen; such men are not few, Verily if a person owns camels, or cattle or flocks and does not set aside the *zakah* on them, these camels, cattle, and flocks will return on the day of resurrection bigger and fatter than they ever were and will butt him with their horns and trample him with their hoofs

---

2. See *Surah* II: 40, 77, 104, 172, 277, etc. Prayer and almsgiving are mentioned side by side in the Qur'an no less than twenty-two times.
3. Al-Bukhari, Imam: 1.
4. *Surah* IX: 34.

over and over again until all the people are judged.' "[5] Since this stricture is related in the two *Sahihs*,[6] it becomes an important part of religion to unfold the mysteries of almsgiving (*zakah*), its obvious and hidden rules, and its outward and inward significance. We shall limit our discussion to those things which the prayer of *zakah* and its recipient should know. These are unfolded under four sections: First, the different kinds of *zakah* and the reasons for its obligatory nature. Second, its inward and outward rules and regulations. Third, the recipient, the conditions which establish his claim, and the etiquette of payment. Fourth, the voluntary almsgiving (*sadaqah*)[7] and its excellence.

5. Cf. Muslim, Zakah: 24, 26, 27; al-Bukhari, Zakah: 44.
6. Al-Bukhari's and Muslim's.
7. The difference between *zakah* and *sadaqah* is that the former is legal and obligatory while the latter is meritorious and voluntary.

SECTION I

On the different kinds of *zakah* and the reasons for its being obligatory, as well as the *zakah* in relation to the various materials on which it is levied. These are of six kinds: 1. on livestocks (*na'am*), 2. on gold and silver (*al-naqdayn*), 3. on merchandise, 4. on buried treasures (*rikaz*) and mines, 5. on land products (*al-mu'ashsharat*), 6. on breaking the fast of Ramadan (*al-fitr*).

1. The Zakah on Livestock

This, as well as the other kinds of *zakah,* is not obligatory except on every free Moslem. That he be an adult and sane is not a prerequisite. In fact the *zakah* is obligatory on minors and the insane. These are the conditions for a person's liability to the *zakah*. Those which render the property liable are five: that it be livestock, maintained on pasturing, in the possession of its owner for at least one uninterrupted year, equivalent to a certain minimum (*nisab*), and wholly owned [by the individual].

The first condition is that the property should be livestock, since only camels, cattle and flocks are liable to the *zakah*, whereas horses, mules, donkeys and the cross-breed of deer and sheep are exempt therefrom.

The second condition is pasturing. Livestock maintained on fodder are not liable to the *zakah*. Again if they were maintained on pasturing a part of the time and fed on fodder the rest of the time, they would be exempted from the *zakah* because of the need to provide for them.

The third condition is possession for [at least] a period of one uninterrupted year. The Apostle of Allah said, "No *zakah* is due on anything until it is in one's possession [for at least] one year."[8] An exception from this rule is the

8. Abu-Dawud, *Zakah*: 5.

produce of property. To it is applied the same rule which governs the property and is liable to the *zakah* because its source [i.e. the original property] has been in the possession of the owner for one uninterrupted year. If during the year the property is sold or given away, the year's possession is interrupted [and the liability to *zakah* falls].

The fourth condition is the whole and complete ownership of the property and freedom of action therein. Consequently, mortgaged livestocks are liable to the *zakah* because the owner himself has been responsible for the sequestration. But lost and confiscated things are not liable to the *zakah* unless they are retrieved, at which time the amount due on them for the previous period must be paid. If the person were indebted to the amount of his capital, he would not be liable to the *zakah* because he is not rich enough, as to be rich is to have a surplus.

The fifth condition is that the property be equal to a certain minimum [which varies with the kind of property on which the *zakah* is levied].

Camels. No *zakah* is due on less than five camels, on which is levied a sheep in its second year or a goat in its third year. On ten camels two goats are levied, on fifteen camels three goats, on twenty camels four goats, and on twenty-five camels a yearling she-camel (*bint mikhad*) which is in its second year of age. If the person did not have among his camels a yearling she-camel then a he-camel in the third year of its age (*ibn labun*) would be taken instead, although the person might be able to buy a yearling she-camel. On thirty-six camels a she-camel in the third year of its age (*bint labun*) is levied; on forty-six camels a she camel in the fourth year of its age (*hiqqah*) is levied; on sixty-one camels a she-camel in the fifth year of its age (*jadha'ah*); on seventy-six camels two she-camels in the third year of their age; on ninety-one camels two she-camels in the fourth year of their age; and on one hundred and twenty-one camels three she-camels in the third year of their age. When their number reaches one hundred and thirty-one camels the scale becomes fixed: for every fifty camels a she-camel in the fourth year of its age is levied, and for every forty camels a she-camel in the third year of its age.

Cattle. No *zakah* is due on less than thirty bulls and cows, on which is levied a calf in the second year of its age (*tabi'*). On forty bulls and cows a cow in the third year of its age (*musinnah*) is levied, and on sixty bulls and cows two calves in the second year of their age. Beyond that the scale becomes fixed: for every forty bulls and cows a cow in the third year of its age is levied, and for every thirty bulls and cows a calf in the second year of its age.

Flock. No *zakah* is due on less than forty sheep and goats, on which one ewe in the second year of its age or one goat in the third year of its age is levied. No *zakah* is due on any more until the number reaches one hundred and twenty-one sheep and goats for which three ewes are levied. When the number reaches four-hundred, four ewes are levied. Beyond this number the scale becomes fixed and for every one hundred sheep and goats one ewe is levied.

The rules which governs the almsgiving (*sadaqah*)[9] of two in partnership (*khalitayn*) is the same as that which governs the *sadaqah* of the sole owner. Thus if two individuals owned forty sheep together [the *zakah*] due on them is one ewe; and if three individuals owned one hundred and twenty ewes in partnership among themselves the *zakah* due on them all is one ewe. Partnership of neighbours, in its liability to the *zakah*, is exactly like common partnership (*khultat al-shuyu*), although it is required that their sheep should be herded together in the same place, taken to drink [192] together [at the same water-hole or well], milked together, graze together in the same pasture, and their mating be carried at the same time and place. Above all the partners should be of the people of the *zakah* [i.e. free Moslems], for the

9. Used here as a synonym of *zakah*.

partnership of the Moslem with the *dhimmi* and the slave who has ransomed himself (*mukatab*)[10] is without the law.

To give as *zakah* a younger camel than the one prescribed by law is permissible, provided the camel given is not younger than a yearling (*bint mikhad*), although the person should make amends for the age of the camel: a camel one year younger than the prescribed age requires two ewes or twenty dirhams compensation; one two years younger, four ewes or forty dirhams. He may also give as *zakah* camels older than the prescribed age as long as they do not go beyond the fifth year of their age (*jadha'ah*). [When camels older in years than the prescribed age have been given as *zakah*], the owner is entitled to [differential] compensation and can collect it from the treasury officials.

No sick camel may be accepted as *zakah* when one sound camel is found among the herd on which the *zakah* is due. From among thorough-bred camels a thorough-bred is collected and from among the half breed, a half-breed. No sheep fattened for slaughtering and eating or gravid may be taken as *zakah*. Likewise no ewe which has just brought forth, or a male, or the best among the flock may be taken.

2. The Zakah on Land Products

The second kind of *zakah* is that which is levied on land products (*al-ma'ashsharat*). The tithe is due on every edible plant when its amount reaches eight hundred manehs. No *Zakah* is due on any amount less than eight hundred manehs. Likewise no *zakah* is due on fruits and cotton but it is due on dates and raisins. To be liable to the *zakah* their amount should not be less than eight hundred manehs and they should be dried dates and raisins, not fresh dates and grapes.

10. Cf. *Surah* XXIV: 33 *Kitabak*, literally "writing," is a form of buying oneself free. It is a contractual liberation where the slave pays his owner a certain equivalent in two or three instalments. The owner is the *mukatib* and the slave is the *mukatab*. The latter alone can annul the contract if he wishes.

Fresh dates and grapes become dried dates and raisins after a process of drying.

In common partnership the property of the one partner supplements that of the other [and the *zakah* is due on the sum of the two]. For example in a vineyard which is owned in common by several heirs and the crop of which amounts to eight hundred manehs of raisins, eighty manehs of raisins are due on all of them together, each to pay in proportion to his share. This, however, does not hold in the partnership among neighbours.

An amount of wheat may not be supplemented with another of barley in order to raise it to the minimum (*nisab*) liable to the *zakah* but an amount of barley may be supplemented with thin-husked barley because they are of the same species.

The quality of the *zakah* due on land products is as follows: dry dates, dry raisins, and dry grains are accepted as *zakah*. Neither grapes nor fresh dates are accepted unless an epidemic should befall the trees and demand, for the sake of the general welfare, that they be cut down before their fruit is ripe. In that event fresh dates, [for example], may be collected--nine measures will be set aside for the owner, and on measure for the poverty-stricken. That the division of property is [equivalent to] the selling [of it] does not prevent such division, rather it is permissible because of necessity.

The *zakah* is due at the time when the fruits become ripe and the grains harden; it is actually collected after the crop has been dried and sifted.

3. The Zakah on Gold and Silver

When a year elapses with two hundred Makkan dirhams of sterling silver [in the possession of a person], the *zakah* due on them will be five dirhams, which is one-forth of ten percent. Anything above that, though it may be only a dirham, follow the same ratio [of one dirham for every forty or one fortieth for each dirham].

The minimum amount (*nisab*) of gold liable to the *zakah* is twenty Makkan miskal of pure gold, on which is due one-fourth of ten percent. The same proportion holds for anything above the minimum, but no *zakah* is due if the minimum were short of one grain. A person possessing counterfeit money is liable to the *zakah* if the pure metal it contains is equivalent to the required minimum. The *zakah* is due on gold and silver bullion as well as on forbidden gold and silver luxuries such as gold and silver vessels and the gold coaches of [rich] men. On the other hand the *zakah* is not due on permissible luxuries. It is also due on the debt of a solvent person capable of paying his debt, in which event it is due at the time of payment. If the payment of the debt has been set for a deferred date, the *zakah* is not due until that date is come.

4. The Zakah on Merchandise

The *zakah* on merchandise, like that on gold and silver [is one-fourth of then percent for the year]. The year, however, is reckoned from the time of the person's possession of the gold and silver with which he has purchased the goods, provided the money was up to the minimum liable to the *zakah*. If the money were below the minimum, or if the person should purchase some goods with the intention of selling them for profit, then the year would be reckoned from the time of the purchase.

The *zakah* is paid with the currency of the land and in terms of the same currency is its value calculated. If the money with which the goods were purchased belonged to a certain monetary unit, and equalled exactly the minimum liable to the *zakah* (*nisab*) it would be better to calculate the *zakah* on the basis of the monetary unit with which the purchase was made than on that of the currency of the land.

If a person decides to invest a part of his income, the year will not be reckoned until he actually purchases something with it, for the mere intent to invest is not enough. If, before the year elapses, the person drops his intention of investing, the obligation to pay the *zakah* likewise drops. It is, however, better to pay the *zakah* for that year.

Whatever profit may accrue at the end of the year is liable to the *zakah* through the year of the capital, and will not have a special year reckoned for it as is the case with the increase of [camels, cattle, and flocks].

As to money-changers, the continuity of the year on the basis of which the *zakah* due on their money is calculated is not interrupted by the exchange of the money to and fro among them as it is interrupted with exchange of other kinds of merchandise.

The *zakah* due on the profits which accrue to the money-lender is due on the lender himself, i.e. on his share of the profit, even before the division of the shares takes place. This is the most regular practice.

5. The Zakah on Buried Treasures and Mines

A buried treasure (*rikaz*) is money interred in the earth sometime during the *Jahiliyah* days and later found in a land to which no one has claimed title during the days of Islam. When such a treasure is discovered, he who finds it is required to pay one-fifth of its value, whether the treasure be gold or silver. The lapse of a one-year period is not required. Likewise no certain minimum need be required, since the fact that one-fifth of its value has been set down as the amount of the *zakah* due on it established its similarity to booty. It is not unusual, however, to require a certain minimum (*nisab*) because the way it is spent is the same as that of the *zakah*. For this reason [the liability to the *zakah*] is confined to gold and silver treasures.

As to mines, no *zakah* is due on any of the metals mined therefrom except gold and silver, on which, according to the best authority, one-fourth of ten percent is due after they have been reduced and purified. Furthermore, a certain minimum (*nisab*) is here required [193]. As to the one-year period two opinions are set forth, [one requiring and the other ignoring it]. But when one-fifth of its value is fixed as the amount of the *zakah* due, the year period is not required.

Two opinions are also set forth regarding the minimum liable to the *zakah*. The more likely is that, in the amount of the *zakah* due on it, it should follow the same rule as merchandise, since it is also a form of profit. In the case of the one-year period it should follow the rule of the land products and therefore no such period is required, since this is the most sensible course. A certain minimum is required in this part as it is required in land products. The safest course is to set aside one-fifth of all buried treasures and mine products regardless of their amount and irrespective of whether or not they are gold or silver, in order to avoid these uncertain distinctions and differences, all of which are conjectural views and almost invariably contradictory. It is, therefore, dangerous to lay down fast and strict rules, especially because of the contradictory nature of these conjectures.

6. The Zakah on Breaking the Fast of Ramadan

The *zakah* on breaking the fast of Ramadan (*al-fitr*) is on the authority of the word of the Apostle of Allah,[11] obligatory upon every Moslem from whose food and the food of his dependants, on the day of *al-fitr* and the night before, a measure, measured with that of the Apostle of Allah, is left over. The measure of the Apostle of Allah was equivalent to two and two-thirds manehs. This he should set aside from whatever food he has been eating or from any superior food. If he were feeding on wheat he may not set aside [a measure] of barley [for the *zakah*], and if he were feeding on several kinds of grains he should select the best and from it set

11. Cf. al-Nasa'i, *zakah*: 30; al-Bukhari, *zakah*: 71-76.

aside the *zakah*. But of whatever grain he sets aside the *zakah* it will be sufficient.

The *zakah* on the breaking of the fast of Ramadan (*al-fitr*) is expended in the same way as that of the other properties, and each of the various beneficiaries should be included. It is not permissible to offer either flour or parched barley as *zakah*. Furthermore it is obligatory upon every Moslem to pay the *zakah* on the breaking of the fast of Ramadan for his wife, slaves, children, and every relative dependent on him, i.e. those relatives whose support is obligatory upon him, such as his father, mother, and children. The Apostle said, "On breaking the fast of Ramadan, give the *sadaqah*[12] on behalf of those whom ye support."[13] In case the slave is jointly possessed by two partners the *sadaqah* is obligatory upon both. It is, however, not obligatory to pay it on behalf of an unbelieving slave. If a wife should independently set aside her own *sadaqah*, her *sadaqah* will be sufficient. Nevertheless, the husband may set aside the *sadaqah* on behalf of his wife without her permission. If, after paying the *sadaqah* of his immediate dependants, a person can still afford it, he should proceed to the *sadaqah* of those next in order beginning with the closest whose claim to his support is the most evident. The Apostle of Allah has given the child's claim for support precedence over the wife's, and the wife's over that of the servant.[14]

The knowledge of these rules of jurisprudence is indispensable to him who wishes to be independent of others. He may, however, be confronted with unusual situations not within the scope of this discussion, in which event he should depend upon expert legal opinion having at first fortified himself with this knowledge.

---

12. *Sadaqah* is used here interchangeably with *zakah*.
13. Unidentified.
14. Cf. al-Nasa'i, *zakah*: 54, where the claim of the wife is given precedence over that of the child.

SECTION II

On the Payment of the Zakah and the Inward and Outward Rules which Govern that Payment

Know that the payer of the *zakah* should observe five things:

1. Intention, which means that the person should purpose in his heart the payment of the ordained *zakah*, but he does not have to specify the property for which he pays the *zakah*. Thus if he had some property under absentee ownership and, on paying the *zakah* due on it, said, "This is paid for the property which I own under absentee ownership, provided that property is safe otherwise let this be a supererogatory deed," his action will be permissible, because he did not specify what the property was. This will be the rule when a property is referred to in general terms.

The intention of the guardian takes the place of that of the insane and the minor. The intention of the magistrate takes the place of that of the owner who has refused to pay the *zakah*, although only as far as the outward forms of this world are concerned. As far as the hereafter is concerned the intention of the magistrate does not take the place of that of the owner who has refused to pay the *zakah*; on the contrary the latter will continue to be held responsible for it until he resumes its payment.

If the owner should intrust an agent with the payment of the *zakah* and, at the time of intrusting, the agent purposes himself to do so, or intrust the agent with the intention, he would fulfil the requirement thereof, because to intrust the agent with the intention is itself an intention.

2. Promptness in paying the *zakah* at the end of each year and on breaking the fast of Ramadan (*al-fitr*). In the case of the latter he should not delay its payment beyond the feast of Ramadan. It is due as soon as the sun sets on the last day of Ramadan, and if one wishes to be very prompt he may pay it during the month of Ramadan, sometime between the first and the last day of the month. Whoever delays the payment of the *zakah*, although he is able to be prompt, sins. Furthermore, if he had been able to pay the *zakah* but delayed to do so and subsequently his property was destroyed, the obligation to pay it will not be removed from him. But if he delayed its payment because no beneficiaries were present to receive it and subsequently his property was destroyed, the obligation to pay the *zakah* will be removed from him.

To pay the *zakah* in advance is permissible provided it is done after the minimum liable to the *zakah* has been obtained and the one-year period has already elapsed. It is, however, permissible to pay the *zakah* of two-years in advance. If the *zakah* is paid in advance and then, before the end of the year, the poor man [who is the beneficiary] should die, or apostate, or grow independently wealthy, or if the property of the owner should be destroyed or he himself die, the sum which had been paid in advance would not constitute a *zakah* and cannot be refunded unless it had been so stipulated at the time of payment. Therefore, let him who pays the *zakah* in advance keep in mind how things may end and watch for a safe outcome.

3. That no substitute based on the value of the *zakah* be offered in its stead. The stipulated *zakah* itself should be set aside and offered. Thus silver (*waraq*) will not take the place of gold, nor gold the place of silver, even though the substitute may exceed that for which it was substituted.

Perhaps some of those who do not understand the purpose of al-Shafi'i may be inclined to be lenient and permit the substitution of one thing for the other on the ground that the main purpose of the whole thing is satisfying the need. But how far is this from the true knowledge of the law. For while satisfying the need is one of its purposes, it is in no way the sole purpose. Rather the purposes of the law are three. [194] These are:

The first purpose of the law is pure devotion (*ta'abbud manad*) not affected by personal considerations or desires. This is, for example, like the throwing of the pebbles at the three *Jamrahs*:[15] no benefit is derived by the *Jamrah* from the falling prebbles. In this case the main purpose of the law is the trial of man through action, in order that he may show his servitude and bondage to Allah by means of acts which [in themselves] have no rational meaning. For acts which [in themselves] have rational meaning are transacted by the aid of the mind which urges man to do them. Consequently, rational acts do not reveal man's complete servitude and bondage to Allah. Real bondage to Allah, however, is revealed through [blind] obedience to His commandments and not through obedience for some other reason. Thus most of the activities of [the pilgrims during] the pilgrimage are, in themselves, void of any rational significance. For this reason, the Apostle, when in the sacred state (*ihram*), said, "With zeal I obey thee O Lord, and through the pilgrimage I display my devotion and servitude." This he did in order to show that man proves his bondage to Allah through blind obedience to His commandments regardless of whether or not they are agreeable to him and irrespective of his desire and inclination to obey them.

The second purpose of the Law is a rational benefit

15. During the pilgrimage, when the pilgrims reach the valley of Mina, each one of them is expected to throw seven small pebbles, which he has already picked up at Muzdalifah, at each of the three heaps (sing. *jamrah*) symbolic of stoning Satan. There are three *Jamrahs*, *al-ula* (the first), *al-wusta* (the middle), and the last which is known as that of *al-'aqabah*. Cf. al-Bukhari: al-Hajj: 134-138; Ibrahim Rif'at, *Mir'at al-Haramayn*, (Cairo, 1925), vol. I, pp. 328-329.

rather than pure devotion, like, for example, honouring human debts and restoring to men whatever was forcibly taken from them. Thus there is not a single offence in which the act itself, as well as the motive, is not taken into consideration. Furthermore whenever the right is restored to its owner or a substitute indemnity agreeable to him has been paid, the demand of the law is fulfilled, and its claims are consequently dropped.

These two purposes of the law are free of complications and their comprehension is readily shared by all men.

The third purpose of the law is composite embracing the former two, namely the benefit of mankind and the trial of man by means of [the yoke of] bondage. Consequently therein is combined acts of pure devotion like the throwing of the pebbles, and human benefits like the restoration of [violated] rights. The latter is, in itself, rational. But if it is ordained by the law, it becomes imperative that the two purposes be combined. Never, however, should the subtler of the two purposes, namely devotion and servitude, be overlooked on account of the more apparent, [namely human benefit and advantage]. More likely the subtler of the two is the more important.

Of this last kind, [i.e. the third], is the *zakah.* No one awoke to this fact except al-Shafi'i. The part of [the *zakah* which is spent on] the poverty-stricken serves the purpose of satisfying the need. This is quite clear and is readily understood. On the other hand the requirements of devotion are fulfilled through carrying our the details which are connected with the *zakah.* In this regard the *zakah* has become an inseparable companion of prayer and the pilgrimage, it being one of the [five] pillars of Islam. No doubt man has to exert some effort in distinguishing the various kinds of his possessions and setting aside a portion of each and finally distributing what he had set aside around eight different groups of [beneficiaries] as will be discussed later. To make concessions on this point will not mitigate the benefits due to the poverty-stricken but will certainly militate against devotion. That devotion is intended in the *zakah* is evidenced by the specific treatment of the different kinds of the *zakah* by the law. These specifications we have discussed under points of dispute in books of jurisprudence. One of the clearest of these specifications is where the law specifically ordains that the *zakah* for every five camels is one ewe, thereby substituting the ewe for the camel but not permitting the substitution of gold and silver. Were this to be explained on the result of the scarcity of gold and silver money among the Bedouins, the explanation would be rendered inadequate as soon as it is recalled that the Apostle has stipulated that the sum of twenty dirhams or two ewes should be given in compensation when the age of the camel given as *zakah* is younger than what it should be.[16] Why then did the Apostle not mention in connection with the compensation required the amount of shortage in the value, and why did he value it at twenty dirhams or two ewes if garments and vessels of whatever kind were all of the same value as substitutes?

These as well as other similar specifications indicate that the *zakah* has not been left void of devotional significance, but unlike the pilgrimage which is purely devotional, embraces both [the rational benefits and the devotional acts]. But whereas feeble minds fail to comprehend complicated things, errors have arisen in this field.

4. That the *sadaqah* should not be transferred from one town to another. For in every town the eyes of the poor look towards the money collected therein for relief; and the transfer of that money to other towns brings disappointment to those who expected aid therefrom. According to one opinion, however, the transfer is permissible. But it is better to avoid anything which may cause dissension. Consequently, let the *zakah* be spent in the town wherein it was collected. when this is observed it will no longer be wrong to spend the *zakah* on such strangers as may be within that town.

16. See above, p.8.

5. That the payer of the *zakah* should divide the sum which he pays among the different groups of beneficiaries found in his home-town. To include all the different groups of beneficiaries is obligatory, which thing is proved by the words of Allah when He said, "But alms (*sadaqat*) are only to be given to the paupers and the poor, and those who collect them, and to those whose hearts are reconciled [to Islam], and those in captivity, and those in debt, and those who are on Allah's path, and for the wayfarers;--an ordiance this from Allah, for Allah is knowing and wise."[17] This resembles the saying of the sick man that one third of his possession is for the paupers and the poor, and consequently this demands settlement through transfer. As for the act of worship care should be taken not to rush through them in a superficial manner.

Of the eight groups of beneficiaries two, namely those whose hearts are reconciled [to Islam][18] and the collectors of the *zakah*, have disappeared in most lands, while four still universally exist. These are the paupers, the poor, those in debt, and the travellers, i.e. the wayfarers. Two groups, namely the warriors and those in captivity (*al-mukatabun*), are still to be found in some lands. Thus if five groups of beneficiaries were found in one place, the payer of the *zakah* should divide it among them in equal or almost equal parts, and should allot to each one part. He then should divide each part into three or more equal or unequal portions. Nevertheless, he is not compelled to divide each part equally among the members of the one group of beneficiaries, but may divide it, if he wishes, into ten or even twenty portions, in which case the share of each individual within the one group will necessarily diminish. The division of the *zakah* among the different groups should not be tampered with:

17. *Surah* IX: 60.
18. *Al-mu'allafah qulubuhum*; see *Surah* IX: 60. These were petty Arab chiefs with whom Muhammad made terms after the battle of Hunayn (A.H. 8/ A.D. 629), in order to secure their aid. See *Sirah*. p.880.

nothing should be taken from the one and added to the other but all should be equal. The share of each group should not be divided into less than three portions. Thus if the amount of the *zakah* due for breaking the fast of Ramadan were one measure of any grain and there were five groups of beneficiaries in the town, the payer, [on the basis of at least three portions within each group], should divide the *zakah* among fifteen men. Should one man be left out and not receive his portion, the payer, if he can afford it, should supply that portion from his own property. But if this were not possible because of the meagerness of the *zakah*, a number of those men who are liable to the *zakah* should pool their dues and then hand them over to the beneficiaries so that they might divide them among themselves. [195] 'Resort to this course of action is indispensable.

On the Details of the Inward Rules of the Zakah

Know that he who seeks the road of the hereafter through the *zakah* has certain duties to fulfil. These are as follows:

The first duty is to understand the reason why the *zakah* is obligatory, to comprehend its significance, to find out how it constitutes a criterion wherewith man's devotion to Allah is tested and tried, and finally why it has been made one of the [five] pillars of Islam although it is merely a financial transaction and does not form a part of bodily worship. This has three significations.

To repeat the two words of the *shahadah* is an obligation necessary for the acknowledgement of the unity of Allah and witness to His oneness. As a prerequisite of man's complete loyalty to Allah he should banish from his heart every love except the One, the Single, since love tolerates no division of affection. Furthermore the verbal profession of the unity of Allah is of little value by itself. The degree of the person's love is tested when he parts with his beloved. Property and wealth are much loved by all people because they are the means by which they enjoy the pleasures of this world, and because of them they love life and hate death, although through it they will meet [Allah] the beloved. As a proof of the truthfulness of their claim that they love Allah they have renounced property and wealth, the objects of their [earthly] attention and devotion. For this reason Allah said, "Verily, of the faithful hath Allah bought their persons and their substance, on condition of Paradise for them [in return]."[19] This is done by means of toil and labour of Allah, by giving up oneself to His service because of one's longing to meet Him. But giving up wealth is easier than giving up oneself. As people read in this the giving away of wealth and property, they were divided into three different groups. One group of men accepted the unity of Allah and fulfilled [the terms of] their covenant[20] renouncing all their wealth and property and storing for themselves neither gold nor silver. Consequently, they refused to concern themselves with the obligation of the *zakah* and that they were expected to pay it, so that when one of them was asked about the *zakah* due on two-hundered dirhams be replied, "The law ordains that the common folk pay five dirhams [as the *zakah* due on two-hundred], but we have to give away all." For this reason Abu Bakr gave away all his possessions and 'Umar gave away half of his. Thereupon the Apostle asked 'Umar, "What have you left for your family?" 'Umar replied, "As much as I have given away." The Apostle then asked Abu-Bakr, "And what have you left for your family?" Abu-Bakr replied, "[The protection of] Allah and His Apostle." The Apostle said, "The difference between you both is the same as the difference between your replies. Verily al-Siddiq has fulfilled his covenant completely, withholding nothing unto himself except Allah and His Apostle."[21]

---

19. *Surah* IX: 112.
20. Cf. *Surah* II:172.
21. Cf. al-Darimi, *Zakah* 28; al-Tirmidhi, Manaqib: 16.

The members of the second group rank lower than those of the first. They withhold their wealth for the hour of need and until the season of giving arrives. Their purpose in saving and storing their wealth is to be able to spend according to their needs, though without extravagance, and to give away for charity whatever is left after they had satisfied their need. In giving, these men do not limit themselves to the *Zakah* but go beyond its fixed amount. In fact some of the followers (*al-tabi'un*), such as al-Nakha'i, al-Sha'bi, 'Ata' and Mujahid, have said that a man's wealth was subject to other [impositions] besides the *zakah*?", Thus al-Sha'bi, having been asked, "Is a man's wealth subject to other [impositions] besides the *zakah*?" said, "Yes. Have you not heard the words of Allah, 'And for the love of Allah distributeth his wealth to his kindred'? "[22] These same men have been guided in this by the words of Allah, "And give alms of that with which we have supplied them;"[23] and "And expend [in the cause of Allah] out of that with which we have supplied you;"[24] claiming that neither of these two verses has been abrogated by that of the *zakah*[25]. Rather they are part of the obligations of one Moslem towards another. In other words whenever a wealthy Moslem comes across one who is needy, he should relieve his want regardless of the fact that he has already paid the *zakah*. In this connection, the correct course, according to jurisprudence, is that the relief of a pressing need is a *fard kifayah*, because the life of a Moslem should not be sacrificed.

It may be said, however that a wealthy Moslem is under no obligation to surrender any of his wealth for the relief of want except in the form of a loan, and that he is not under any compulsion to give any of it away once he has fulfilled the requirement of the *zakah*. It may also be said

---

22. *Surah* II: 172.
23. *Surah* XXII: 36.
24. *Surah* LXIII: 10.
25. I.e. *Surah* IX: 60.

that he should give away of his wealth for the relief of want but not in the form of a loan. In other words it is not permissible for him to place the poor under the obligation of accepting the loan [and the obligation of paying it back]. Differences of opinion on this question do exist. [To relieve want by] loans [rather than by outright gifts] is to descend to the lowest rank of the common folk which is the rank of the third group.

The members of this third group confine themselves solely to the fulfillment of that which is obligatory; they add nothing to it and take nothing away from it. This is, indeed, the lowest rank to which the common folk have confined themselves because of their niggardliness, and because of their strong love for money and their lukewarm love for the hereafter. Said Allah, "If He were to ask you for your property and to press you for it, ye would be niggardly."[26] (To press you means to urge you). And what a difference is there between a servant from whom [Allah] has purchased his wealth and soul in return for Paradise and another whom [Allah] does not urge because of his niggardliness! This, therefore, is one of the meanings of the commandment of Allah to His servants to give their wealth away.

The second meaning is to purify oneself from the stigma of niggardliness which is one of the destructive matters of life. The Apostle said, "Three things in life are destructive: sordid avarice, vehement passion, and self-conceit."[27] Allah also said, "And whoso is preserved from his own covetousness, these are the prosperous."[28] We shall discuss in the Quarter on the Destructive Matters of Life in what way it is destructive as well as the manner of avoiding it.

The stigma of niggardliness is removed by the practice of giving money away, since the love of a thing is overcome

26. *Surah* XLVII: 39.
27. Al-Manawi, *Fayd al-Qadir, Sharh al-Jami' al-Saghir*, vol. III (Cairo, 1938), p.307.
28. *Surah* LIX: 9, LXIV: 16.

by compelling oneself to stay away from it until abstention becomes habitual. According to this meaning the *zakah* is purity because it purifies the person who fulfils it from the destructive impurities of niggardliness. The extent to which the person if purified from the stigma of niggardliness is proportional to the amount of his giving and the degree of his pleasure in giving and in his delight in spending in the cause of Allah.

The third meaning is gratitude for the blessings of Allah, for He has blessed man in his own self and in his possessions. The bodily acts of worship [196] are man's gratitude for the bodily blessings which Allah has bestowed upon him, while the financial acts of worship are his gratitude for the financial gifts. How vile and ungrateful then is the person who sees a poverty-stricken man in dire distress and need but does not extend to him a helping hand by giving him one-fourth of ten percent or ten percent of his wealth as a sign of his gratitude of Allah for sparing him the necessity of begging and visiting it upon others instead.

The second duty concerns the time of payment. One of the signs of etiquette among religious people is to pay [the *zakah*] before it is already due, in order to show their desire to conform willingly to the law by bringing [relief and] happiness to the hearts of those in poverty, losing no time therein lest unforeseen obstacles arise and prevent them from doing good; and because of their knowledge that in delay are many evils, and that man exposes himself to [the fruits of] disobedience whenever he delays the payment of the *zakah* beyond the appointed time. Whenever the impulse for doing good makes itself felt inwardly, the person should seize the opportunity [and hearken unto it] for in so doing he would join the company of heaven, since at that time "the heart of the believer is between two of the fingers of the Merciful Allah." But how quickly does the heart change its position. For Satan threatens [men] with poverty and invites them to commit turpitude and evil. He has a company that goes after the company of heaven. Consequently, let man seize the opportunity and appoint a definite month for the payment the *zakah* if he were wont to pay it annually; and let him endeavour to have that month fall in the best part of the year, so that he may increase in the favour of Allah and his *zakah* be multiplied double fold. Such a month would be *al-Muharram* because it is the first month of the year and one of the sacred months;[29] or Ramadan in which the Apostle, who was the best of creation, was like the open air free of all impurities.[30] To Ramadan also belongs the excellence of the Night of Power (*Laylat al-Qadr*)[31] as well as that of being the month in which the Qur'an was revealed. Mujahid was wont to say, "Say not Ramadan, because Ramadan is one of the names of Allah; but say ye the month of Ramadan."[32] Dhu-al-Hijjah is another of the months which claim great excellence since besides being a sacred month, it also boasts of the greater pilgrimage (*al-hajj al-akbar*)[33] the appointed days (*al-ayyam al-ma'lumat*),[34] which are the first ten days of the same month, and the numbered days (*al-ayyam al-ma'dudat*) which are the days of orientation (*ayyam al-tashriq*)[35]. The most excellent days of the month

---

29. During which fighting was unlawful. These were Dhu-al-Qa'dah, Dhu-al-Hijjah, al-Muharram, and Rajab.
30. Cf. al-Bukhari, Manaqib: 23.
31. The night of the day on which Muhammad received his call. It was later fixed towards the end of Ramadan A.D. 610, twelve years before the Hijrah. See *Surah* XCVII: al-Bukhari, Bad' al-Wahy.
32. That Ramadan is one of the names of Allah is based on a weak tradition which I failed to locate.
33. To distinguish it from the lesser pilgrimage, both of which will be discussed in the Book on the Pilgrimage.
34. Being the first ten days of Dhu-al-Hijjah, the last of which is the day of sacrifice. *Surah* XXII: 29.
35. These are the three days next after the day of sacrifice which is the tenth day of Dhu-al-Hijjah. They are now days of rest after the peripatetic performance of the last four. Evidently, they had pre-islamic antecedents. The *tashriq* may either mean turning eastward in worship, or drying up the blood of the sacrifice in the torrid sun of Makkah. It may also mean sunrise-prayer, to which meanign I incline. Cf. *Surah* II: 199.

of Ramadan are the last ten, and the most excellent of Dhu-al-Hijjah are the first ten.

The third duty is secrecy. It is farther removed from the desire to be seen and heard. The Apostle said, "The most excellent *sadaqah* is the secret effort of one of meagre resources to relieve a poverty-stricken individual."[36] One of the learned men said, "Three things are among the precious works of righteousness, one of which is to give alms (*sadaqah*) in secret."[37] This same saying has been related as tradition.[38] The Apostle also said, verily when a man does some thing [good] in secret Allah will record it down to his credit in secret; if he reveals it, it will be transferred from the list of the good works done in secret to that of the good works done openly; if he talks about it, it will be stricken out from both list and put down in that of the works of hypocrisy."[39] And again in the well-authenticated (*mashhur*)[40] tradition, he said, "Seven people will Allah cover with His shadow on the day when there will be no shadow but His; one of these seven is a man who gives alms but his left hand does not know what his right does."[41] In another tradition he said, "Alms given in secret turn away the wrath of Allah."[42] Said Allah, "But if ye hide it [i.e. almsgiving] and bring it to the poverty-stricken, then it is better for you."[43] The advantage of secrecy in giving alms is salvation from the evils of the desire to be seen and heard. The Apostle said, "Allah will not accept the gift of the braggart, the hypocrite, and the person who is always reminding others of the favours he has done for them."[44] For he who brags about his alms seeks

---

36. Cf. Abu-Dawud, *Zakah*: 40.
37. Cf. Matt. VI: 3,4.
38. Unidentified.
39. Unidentified,
40. A tradition is *mashhur* when it is vouched for by more than two Companions.
41. Al-Bukhari, Adhan: 36; cf. Matt. VI: 3,4.
42. Cf. al-Trimidhi, *Zakah*: 28.
43. *Surah* II: 273.
44. Unidentified.

to be known and heard, and he who gives his alms in the presence of crowds desires to be seen and recognized; while secrecy and silence are the best protection against [such temptations].

Some have emphasized the excellence of secrecy in giving alms to an extent where they endeavour to conceal the identity of the benefactor from the beneficiary. Some were wont to place their alms in the hand of a blind man; others used to throw them in the path of the poverty-stricken or in his sitting place where he could see them without seeing the giver; others were in the habit of hiding them in the garments of the poor while he was fast asleep; and others used to convey them to the poverty-stricken indirectly through an intermediary so that the identity of the giver might remain unknown. The intermediary, in turn, was charged with silence and warned not to divulge the identity of the giver. These men took all this trouble to insure that the wrath of Allah has been turned away from them and to avoid the evils of being seen and heard. Whenever it is not possible to give the alms without being known by some one, it is better to give the alms over to an agent who would pass them to the poor whose identity should remain unknown to the benefactor; for in knowing the identity of the poor who had received the alms lies both the desire to be known and the evil practice of reminding the poor of the favour done to him, while in knowing only the intermediary, there lies nothing but the desire to be known.

Whenever the giver's aim in giving is fame, his good deed will prove useless since the purpose of the *zakah* is to banish niggardliness and weaken the love of wealth, yet the love of position and rank is more insidious than the love of wealth, and both [197] are destructive in the hereafter. While the quality of niggardliness becomes, so to speak, in the grave a stinging scorpion, the desire to be seen is transformed into a biting viper. Yet man is required to weaken or destroy them in order to avoid their harm or at least lessen it. But whenever, he seeks to be seen and heard, he strengthens, as it were, the viper and weakens the scorpion. To the extent to which he weakens the scorpion, he strengthens the viper. If he had left them as they were, it would have been easier for him [to avoid their harm]. For the strength of these qualities lies in doing according to their demands, and their weakness is found in opposing and contradicting them and in doing contrary to their demands. Thus what use is there in contradicting the demands of niggardliness and bending before the urge of being seen by men hereby weakening the weaker of the two and strengthening the stronger? (The mysteries of these things will be discussed in the Quarter on the Destructive Matters of Life).

The fourth duty is that the giving of alms be made public, if in so doing men are induced to do likewise and give. The giver, however, should, when making public his gift, guard against being seen in the manner which we shall discuss under the treatment of hypocrisy in the Book on that subject. For Allah has said "If ye display your almsgiving, then well is it"[45] This refers to such occasions where display is needed either for the sake of setting an example for giving or because someone has begged for alms in the presence of a great crowd, in which case giving should not be deferred or neglected for fear of being seen. Rather the person should give to him who has begged and try as much as possible to guard himself against being seen. That is because, besides the evils of constantly reminding people of favours done them and the desire to be seen, there is a third thing to be guarded against in connection with the giving of alms in public. This is the fear of disgracing the poverty-stricken, whose feelings may be hurt at being publicly discovered to be needy. But he who begs in public is solely responsible for bringing disgrace upon himself, and as such, there is no danger of hurting his feelings in giving him alms in public. This is like exposing the incontinence of a person who has hitherto concealed it. Such an exposure is forbidden.

45. *Surah*: II, 273.

Likewise, spying at the person and discussing his incontinence in his absence are prohibited. But he who displays his incontinence openly should be punished by spreading the news of his offence among men although, in reality, he is the cause of it all. Of the same meaning are the words of the Apostle when he said, "He who casts off the garment of shame has no protection against calumny."[46] Allah said, "And those who expend in alms, in secret and in public, out of what we have bestowed upon them."[47] He called men to give alms in public, openly, because of the conducive influence which such giving contains. Let man, therefore, be extremely careful in his choice between this beneficial influence and the dangers inherent therein for they vary with the variation of conditions and individuals. Under certain conditions making the giving of alms public is better for some individual. In short any one familiar with the advantages and disadvantages [of giving alms in public] and entertains no wordly ambitions, will readily discern what is better and more fitting under each different condition.

The fifth duty is that man should not make his alms (*sadaqah*) void by taunts and injury. Allah said, "Make not your alms void by reproaches and injury."[48] People have differed in their definition of taunting and injury. Some have said that taunting is to remind people of favours done for them, while injury is to make them public. Sufyan[49] said, "He who resorts to taunting renders his alms void." Thereupon he was asked, "And how does a man resort to taunting?" To which he replied, "By mentioning his alms and discussing them." Others said that taunting is to enslave a person by a gift while injury is to deride him for his poverty. It was also said that taunting is to lord it over a person for having given him something while injury is to upbraid and

46. Unidentified.
47. *Surah* XIII: 22.
48. *Surah* II: 266.
49. Al-Thawri.

rebuke him for begging. The Apostle said, "Allah will not accept the gifts of the person who is always reminding others of the favours he has done for them."[50] In my opinion taunting springs from the [hidden] states and qualities of the heart and then branches out into different concrete forms which manifest themselves through the tongue and the senses. Actually, the giver should deem himself a beneficiary and the poverty-stricken, by virtue of accepting his gifts which are due to Allah, his benefactor. For in this lie man's justification and his salvation from Hell-fire. Had the poverty-stricken declined to accept his gifts, man would have remained under an obligation to give. It is his duty, therefore, to acknowledge that he is under an obligation to the poverty-stricken who has made his hand a substitute for that of Allah in receiving the dues [which man owes to] Allah. The Apostle of Allah said, "Verily, alms fall into the hand of Allah before they fall into the hand of the beggar who receives them."[51] Let man therefore, know that [when he gives alms], he gives them unto Allah while the poor [who receives them] is receiving his livelihood from Allah to whom it was first given. Thus if a person were indebted to another for a certain sum of money, and should turn over the responsibility of its payment to his slave or servant, both of whom are dependent upon him for their livelihood, and then if on paying the debt the slave or the servant should think that he had placed the recipient under an obligation to himself, this would be sheer impudence and ignorance, because the benefactor who deserves the credit is he on whom both the slave and the servant depend for their livelihood, whereas the slave [or the servant] who had made the payment would have done nothing but discharge a debt which the master had incurred, thereby gaining his favour and consequently aiding himself without placing anyone else

50. Unidentified.
51. Unidentified.

under obligation to himself. In fact whenever he understands the three different meanings which we have mentioned in connection with the obligatory nature of the *zakah*, whenever he understands at least one of them, he will realize that he has not done any good except to himself either through expending his wealth to show his love to Allah, or to purify himself from the vice of niggardliness, or to give thanks unto Allah for the blessing of wealth and ask for more.

Whatever the case may be no dealings can exist between him and the poverty-stricken until he deems himself the benefactor. Whenever he succumbs to such folly he manifests the outward [symptoms of] taunting which we have already discussed, namely repeated discussion of ones alms and insistence on making them known, seeking reward from the beneficiary by expecting from him thanks, praise, service, respect, and veneration, and by requiring him to carry out errands for him, pay him homage in assemblies, and agree with him on all subjects. All these are [198] the fruits of taunting. The inward meaning of taunting we have already mentioned.

The outward manifestations of injury are rebuke, derision, rough speech, stern looks, putting to shame by exposure, and all manner of ridicule. Its inward nature wherefrom its outward manifestations spring is made up of two things: the one is man's unwillingness to give up any of his wealth and the extreme pain which it causes him when he parts with any of it. This [attitude] makes a man inevitably short tempered. The second is his belief that he is superior to the poor who, by reason of his need, is inferior. Both these things are the result of ignorance. For he who dislikes to expend one dirham for a thousand is extremely foolish. It is also well known that he expends his wealth in order to receive the favour of Allah and to enjoy His rewards in the hereafter. The wealth which he expends for this purpose is nobler than that which he had spent or may spend to purify himself from the stigma of niggardliness or to give thanks in the hope of receiving more. Whatever you may assume, there is no justification for man's unwillingness [to part with any of his wealth].

The second thing [which makes up the inward nature of injury and wherefrom its outward manifestations spring] is ignorance. For if man would realize the superiority of poverty over wealth he would not despise the poor, but rather would seek his blessing and wish that he were in his position instead; since the righteous among the wealthy would enter Paradise five-hundred years after the poor.[52] For this reason the Apostle said, "By the Lord of the Ka'bah, they shall suffer the greatest loss." Thereupon Abu-Dharr asked, "And who are they [who shall suffer the greatest loss?"] The Apostle replied, "Those who have the most of wealth..." to the end of the tradition.[53] Furthermore, how could he despise the poverty-stricken when Allah has made the latter the source of his profit, since through the labours of the poverty-stricken he earns and accumulates his wealth, hoarding of it according to his need? He has been ordered [by Allah] to give the poverty-stricken in accordance to his need and to withhold from him any surplus which will harm him if it were given to him. The wealthy is, therefore, employed in providing for the poverty-stricken and differs from him by his duty to settle disputes and shoulder responsibilities, and his stewardship over the surplus [of his wealth] until he dies, when his enemies will devour what he has left. Consequently, when man's unwillingness to part with any of his wealth is displaced by gladness and joy for the aid which Allah has given him to fulfil his duty [of paying the *zakah*] and handing it over to the poverty-stricken, so that the poverty-stricken, by accepting the payment, might free him from obligation, injury and its [outward manifestations of] rebuke and stern looks will cease and will

---

52. Cf. al-Tirmidhi, Zuhd: 37.
53. See above, p.3; Muslim, Zakah: 24; al-Bukhari, Zakah: 44.

be replaced by rejoicing, praise, and graceful acceptance of obligation. These then are the causes of taunting and injury.

If you should then say that for a man to see himself as a benefactor is, therefore, [indefinite and] obscure and consequently ask whether or not there is a sign wherewith to test his heart and, [failing to find it], ascertains that he is not a benefactor, then know that such a sign does exist. It is a minute but clear sign and is distinguished in the following manner. The man should confront himself with the following question: Supposing a poverty-stricken man should commit an offence against him or should aid an enemy in a conspiracy against him, would the man's disapproval of and disgust at the poverty-stricken man's behaviour be more intense if the latter had committed his offence after he had received the alms from him than if he had committed it before he had received the alms? If his disapproval and disgust become more intense because the poverty-stricken man has offended against him after receiving alms from him, then the man's giving of alms is not free from the taint of taunting, since he has expected from the proverty-stricken man, after the latter had received his alms, what he has not expected before.

If you should, then say that such an expectation is very indefinite and obscure and that the heart of no one is free from it and ask what remedy may be used for it, then know that it has both an internal and an external remedy. The internal remedy is to know the truths which we have already mentioned concerning the obligatory nature [of the *zakah*] and to realize that the poverty-stricken man, by his acceptance of the *zakah*, enables the benefactor to purify himself [before Allah], and is, therefore, the real benefactor. The external remedy comprises the good works which the man who is under obligation does, since the motives from which works proceed colour the heart with their own nature as will be discussed in the last part of this Book. For this reason some were wont to place the *sadaqah* before the poverty-stricken and, standing before him, beg him to accept it, so that those giving might appear in the form of beggars and to experience the unpleasant feeling of fear lest they be refused. Others used to stretch out their open palms so that the poverty-stricken man might take [the *sadaqah*] therefrom and appear in the role of givers. Both 'A'ishah and Umm-Salamah,[54] whenever they sent a gift or a favour to a poverty-stricken man, used to ask the messenger with whom they sent the gift to remember what good the poverty-stricken man had wished them on receiving their gifts and wish him the same saying, "This wish for his wish, so that our *sadaqah* may be true." They never expected good wishes [in return for their alms] because such wishes are somewhat like a reward. Consequently they responded to every good wish with one like it. The same thing was done by 'Umar ibn-al-Khattab and his son 'Abdullah. Likewise the physicians of the heart (*arbab al-qulub*) used to treat their hearts, since there is no external cure for the heart except these good works which signify self-abasement, humility, and acceptance of obligation; while internally their cure is found in knowledge of the facts which we have already mentioned. The one is from the standpoint of works and the other from that of knowledge. Furthermore, the heart cannot be treated except by means of knowledge and works, a condition in almsgiving corresponding to humility in prayer. This is attested by the words of the Apostle when he said, "Man gains nothing from his prayer except when it is intelligent."[55] This is similar to the words of the Apostle which he said, "Allah will not accept the gifts of a person who is always reminding others of the favours he has done for them."[56] It is also similar to the words of Allah when He said, "Make

---

54. Hind bint-abi-Umayyah, one of the wives of the Prophet; A.H. 59, A.D. 679: see ibn-Qutaybah, p. 67: ibn-Sa'd, vol. VIII, pp. 60-67.
55. Unidentified.
56. Unidentified.

not your alms void by reproaches and injury."[57] The opinion of the jurisprudent that the *sadaqah* is fulfilled regardless of the condition [of knowledge and works according to that knowledge] and that, once given, the person frees himself from the obligation is a different matter altogether, and we have alluded to the meaning of the tradition which purports to support it in the Book on Prayer.

The sixth duty is that man should belittle his gift because if he should make much of it he would be led to feel well-pleased with it, and vanity is one of the destructive matters of life and renders all good works useless. Said Allah, "And on the day of Hunayn[58] when ye were well-pleased with your number it availed you nothing."[59] It is also said that whenever a good work is belittled by man it grows greater in the sight of Allah; on the other hand whenever sin is considered weighty by man it becomes light in the eyes of Allah. It has also been said that a good work is not made perfect except through three things, namely belittling its importance, hastening its execution, and concealing its report [199].

To make much of a gift, however, is distinct from either taunting or injury. For if a person had expended [some of] his wealth for erecting a mosque or building an outpost (*ribat*)[60] he could very easily think much of his donation but he could not possibly taunt or cause injury to anyone. Yet vanity and the practice of making much of one's good works invade all the acts of worship and have no remedy except

---

57. *Surah* IX: 25.
58. At the battle of Hunayn, a valley three miles from Makkah (A.H. 8, A.D. 630) the followers of Muhammad, presuming upon the superiority of their number, 12,000 men, over the enemy who were only 4000 strong, were seized with panic throughout their renks. Order was restored and victory obtained through the bravery and presence of mind of Muhammad and his kindred. See al-Tabari, vol. I, pp. 1654 *seq.*: *Sirah*, p. 840, *seq.*
59. *Surah* IX: 25.
60. For lodging Moslem warriors in the frontier.

in knowledge and works.

Knowledge entails that a person should recognize that ten percent or one fourth of ten percent, [the customary *zakah* rates], is but a little portion of a great amount, [and that by so doing], the person has been content not to go beyond the lowest degree of giving as we have explained under the obligatory nature of the *zakah*. He should, therefore, be ashamed of this little portion rather than proud of it. If on the other hand he should attain the highest degree and give all his wealth, or the greater part of it, [in alms], let him, before priding himself over it, ponder over the source of his wealth and over the purpose of its expenditure. For all his wealth belongs to Allah to whom he is under obligation since Allah has given him all and has aided him in the spending thereof. [Why then should he deem what he expends for Allah much when it all belongs to Allah]?[61] And if his station in life should demand that he consider the hereafter and, therefore, expend his wealth for the sake of reward, why should he make much of his expending that for which he expects manifold reward in the hereafter?

Works, on the other hand, [involve the manner of giving] and require that the person should give because of his sense of shame which he feels for with holding the remainder of his wealth from Allah. Hence the manner of his giving should be one of humility and shame, just like the person who is requested to hand back a deposit but returns one part of it and withholds another. For the whole of [man's] wealth belongs to Allah who prefers that it should be all expended. He did not command His servants to do so because of the difficulty that such a command would cause them because of their niggardliness. Thus He said, "And were He to press you for it, ye would be niggardly."[62]

The seventh duty is that the person should, [when giving], select from his wealth the portion which is best and

---

61. Words in bracets not in B.
62. *Surah* XLVII: 39.

dearest unto him; for Allah is good and accepts nothing but the good. If what he sets aside [for the *zakah*] be taken from wealth secured in a dubious way and his title to it is questionable, then it fails to fulfil the required conditions. In that tradition related by Aban[63] on the authority of Anas we read, "Blessed is the servant who expends from wealth which he has earned without sin." If the portion set apart [for the *zakah*] is not of the best of a man's wealth he will then be guilty of misconduct for he keeps the best for himself or for his servant or for his family and withholds it from Allah, thereby giving preference to others over Allah. If he does the same thing with his guest and offers him the worst food to be found in his house, he will certainly gain his displeasure.

What we have discussed is from the standpoint of Allah, but if man were to view the matter from his own standpoint it would be inconceivable that he would give other the preference, especially since none of his wealth profits him excepting that which he has given in alms, thereby preserving for himself that which would have been lost if he had spent it on himself for an immediate purpose like, for example, eating. It is, therefore, foolish to limit one's attention to immediate things and neglect to store up for the future. Said Allah. "O ye who believe! Bestow alms of the good things which ye have acquired, and of that which we have brought forth for you out of the earth, and choose not the bad for almsgiving, such as ye would not take yourselves except by connivance."[64] In other words they will not accept such bad things for themselves except unwillingly and for fear of shame at its refusal. This is what connivance means. Therefore, prefer not yourselves to Allah by giving him the bad and keeping the good for yourselves.

We also read in the tradition that "one single dirham has

63. Perhaps ibn-abi-'Ayyash; cf. ibn-Sa'd, vol. Vii, pt. 2, p.19.
64. *Surah* II: 269-70

been preferred to a hundred thousand."[65] This obtains whenever man sets the dirham aside from the best portion of his wealth in a spirit of contentment and joy. On the other hand he may set aside a hundred thousand dirhams from a portion of his wealth which he loathes thereby proving that he will not give unto Allah anything which he likes. for the same reason Allah has condemned a group of people who have assigned to Him that which they loathe and abhor. He said, "Yet what they loathe themselves do they assign to Allah; and their tongues utter the lie, that theirs shall be a goodly lot. But beyond a doubt theirs is the Fire."[66] In other words the fire is their reward for assigning to Allah that which they themselves loathe and dislike.

The eighth duty is to seek for his *sadaqah* one worthy of it rather than simply be content that the recipient is one of the rank and file of the eight groups of beneficiaries. For among the rank and file of these eight groups groups are some possessing particular qualities. Let him, therefore, be on the look out for these qualities and, in giving, let him take them into consideration.

These qualities are six in number and are as follows:

First he should seek the pious who have renounced the world and have devoted themselves exclusively to the affairs of the hereafter. The Apostle said, "Do not partake except of the food of a pious man and let no one partake of yours except the pious."[67] This is because the pious is aided by that food to lead a life of piety. Hence by aiding him you would be his partner in his acts of worship. The Apostle also said, "Set your food before the pious and bestow your favours upon the believers."[68] According to another version, "With your substance entertain those whom you love in Allah."[69]

---

65. Unidentified.
66. *Surah* XVI: 64.
67. Cf. al-Tirmidhi, Zuhd: 56; abu-Dawud, Adab: 16.
68. Unidentified.
69. unidentified.

One of the learned was wont to single out the poverty-Stricken Sufis and feed them. On being told that it would be better if he would include all the poverty-stricken in his charity he said, "No! These Sufis are devoting all their energies to Allah; if they should come exposed to any need they might be discouraged or confused. Verily to revive the zeal of one single person devoted to Allah is better than giving alms to a thousand whose concern is this world." This was related to al-Junayd, and he approved of it saying, "Verily this man is one of the saints of Allah," and added, "It is a long long time since I heard words [200] better than these." Sometime later it was related that this same man came upon hard times and decided to close shop. Thereupon al-Junayd sent him some money and said, "Make this your capital and do not close down your shop; verily commerce has no ill-effect on men like you." This man was grocer who charged the poor nothing for the groceries which they perchased at his shop.

Second, the recipient should be one of those who have devoted themselves to knowledge and learning. Such gifts and alms are a [great] help to him in his search after knowledge. And knowledge, when coupled with good intentions, is the noblest form of worship. Thus ibn-al-Mubarak was wont to give his alms exclusively to the devotees of learning. As a result he was told, "If only you would give others as well." He replied, "I know of no rank, next to that of prophecy, which is better or superior to the rank of the learned men. If one of them were to bother himself about his needs he would not be able to devote his time to knowledge or concentrate upon study. Therefore, it is better to give them all the leisure and help them to apply themselves exclusively to knowledge and learning."

Third, that the recipient be true in his piety and honest in his belief in Allah and in the acceptance of His unity. The sign of his belief in Allah and in His unity is to praise Allah and thank Him and to acknowledge that He is the source of his blessing and not attempt to ascribe it to another. He who is most grateful to Allah does this: he acknowledges that Allah is the source of all blessings. In Luqman's testament to his son he said, "Hold not between yourself and your Allah any intermediary benefactor and regard all other benefactors as instruments [in His hands] compelled to execute His will." He who gives thanks to anyone but Allah does not know the Benefactor and does not realize that the intermediary instrument [of benefaction] is under compulsion subject to the will of Allah who has subordinated [the intermediary instruments, i.e. the secondary causes] to the motives (dawa'i) of action and has made the means [of execution] available unto them. Consequently, the giver makes his gift under compulsion, and once Allah has implanted in his heart that his well-being in this world and the next depends upon giving, he cannot neglect it even if he should so desire. When the impulse (*ba'ith*) becomes strong it demands the taking of a definite stand and the rising to immediate action,[70] with the result that a person will be unable to resist or contradict a strong impulse in which there is no room for indecision or hesitation. For it is Allah who creates impulses and arouses them to action; it is He who heals their weaknesses and does away with their indecision. He it is who imposes upon men the task of rising to action according to their impulses. And he who realizes this fact pays no attention except to the cause of causes (*musabbib al-asbab*). Such a realization is of greater value to the giver than all the praise and thanks he may receive, [both] being nothing but chatter which is for the most part useless. [Hence] the opportunity to aid a believing worshipper should not be lost. But he who gives praise when he revives a gift and wishes the giver good, will find fault when it is withheld from him and will curse whenever he despairs of receiving a gift[71] Such persons, however, differ [as to the extent of

70. Another reading has 'and the seizing of opportunity.'
71. In B.C. and mrgin of SM "whenever he is hurt or injured."

their reactions].

It has been related that the Apostle of Allah once sent a gift to one of the poverty-stricken and charged the messenger to [be sure and] remember what the man would say. On receiving the gift sent to him by the Apostle the poverty-stricken man said, "Praise be to God who forgeteth not him who remembereth Him and neglecteth not him who is grateful unto Him." The poverty-stricken man then added, "O Allah! Thou hast not forgotten me; teach me, therefore, not to forget thee." The Apostle of God was informed of this, and he was well pleased and said, "I have known that he would say this. Behold, then, how he centred his attention on Allah alone."[72] At another time the Apostle ordered a certain man saying, "Repent." The man replied, "Before Allah alone I shall repent and not before Muhammad." Thereupon the Apostle said "He has known to whom the prerogative belongs."

When, in connection with the false rumour (*qissat al-ifk*)[73] against 'A'ishah, her innocence was revealed, Abu-Bakr, [her father], told her, "Get up and kiss the head of the Apostle of Allah." But 'A'ishah replied, "No! By the eternal I shall not do that and I shall thank no one except Allah." Thereupon the Apostle said, "Let her alone, O Abu-Bakr."[74] According to another version 'A'ishah told Abu-Bakr, I shall sing the praise of Allah, not yours nor that of your friend."[75]

---

72. Unidentified.
73. The rumour of improper intimacy between 'A'ishah and Safwan ibn-al-Mu'attal, during Muhammad's return from the expedition against the banu-al-Mustaliq (A.H.6/A.D. 627-628), in which he was separated from her for an entire day, which she passed in the company of Safwan, who had found her when accidentally left behind. The scandal was propagated by one Mistah, a relative of 'A'ishah. *Surah* XXIV: 4-26 were revealed to Muhammad shortly afterwards and the innocence of 'A'ishah was therby established. See ibn-Hisham, *Sirah*, pp. 731-740.
74. Cf. al-Bukhari, Shahadat: 15.
75. I.e. Muhammad. Cf. al-Bukhari, Maghazi; 36.

The Apostle did not find fault with what she said although the revelation [of her innocence] reached through the words of the Apostle himself. To see things [independent of Allah] and proceeding from a source other than Him is characteristic of the unbelievers. Thus Allah said, "And when Allah alone is mentioned the hearts of those who believe not in the hereafter is filled with disgust, but when those besides Him are mentioned, lo! they are filled with joy."[76] Consequently, he who does purify his inward soul from [the error of] seeing the secondary causes [201] except as instruments [in the hands of Allah] persists secretly in the sin of associating others with Allah. Let him therefore fear Allah and purify his belief from the defects and blemishes of associating others with Allah.

The fourth quality is [that the recipient] be unknown, having concealed his need, and not much given to complaint and grumble. He should be one of the people of magnanimity who has lost his wealth but still keeps his magnanimous qualities and maintains his poise and self-restraint. Thus has Allah said, "Those who know them not, think them rich because of their modesty. By this their token thou shalt know them--they ask not of men importunately."[77] In other words they do not pester people begging because they are rich in their faith and proud in their fortitude. Such men should be sought by thorough investigation into the lives of religious men in every place and close examination of the inward states of men possessed of goodness and self-restraint. The reward for extending favours to them is manifold the reward of extending it to those who make known their needs and beg openly.

The fifth quality is that the recipient should be one who has to support a family or one disabled through sickness or some other cause, whose state corresponds to that which Allah described when He said, "There are among you the

76. *Surah* XXXIX: 46.
77. *Surah* II: 274.

poverty-stricken, who being shut up to fighting for the cause of Allah, have it not in their power to strike out into the earth [for riches]."[78] In other words they are straitened in the way of the hereafter because of some sickness, or distress, or a change of heart. They are "unable to 'knock about' in the earth" because their wings, [as it were], are clipped and their limbs are tied down with shackles. For these reasons 'Umar was wont to give the people of the house (*ahl-al-hayt*)[79] a whole flock of sheep numbering at least ten sheep. The Apostle himself used to bestow the gift in accordance to the size of the family.[80] 'Umar was once asked about the greatest misfortune and he replied, "A big family and a small wealth."

The sixth is that he should be a relative close of kin so that the gift would be both a *sadaqah* and a favour to the close of kin. A favour to the close kin has countless rewards. 'Ali said, "I had rather give one of my brothers a single dirham than give twenty dirhams in alms; and I had rather give my brother twenty than give away a hundred in alms;" and again, "I had rather give him a hundred dirhams than give a slave his freedom." Both friends and the brethren of good should be given precedence over acquaintances just as relatives are given precedence over non-relatives.

Let, therefore, these details be observed, since they are the required qualities. Each quality has several degrees of which the highest should be sought. If there should be found one who possesses in himself a number of these qualities, that man has taken hold of the greatest treasure and the most valuable booty. Whenever he tries to secure these qualities and is successful in his effort he gains two rewards; but if he fails he earns but one reward. One of his two rewards is the immediate purification of himself from the

---

78. *Surah* II: 274.
79. A tern used in the Qur'an (*Surah* XXXIII: 33) and the tradition Muhammad's household.
80. Ch. Abu-Dawud, Kharaj: 14.

quality of niggardliness and the establishment of the love of Allah in his heart as well as [the will] to endeavour and labour in His worship. These are also the qualities which grow stronger and stronger in his heart and make him long to meet Allah. The second reward is the benefit which he reaps from the prayers and aspirations of the recipient, for the hearts of the righteous exert an immediate and an ultimate influence. If he succeeds [in securing these qualities] the two rewards obtain; but if he fails only the first reward is his. In this manner the reward of him who succeeds in his endeavour is doubled, both is this case and in the others as well.

SECTION III

On the Recipient, the Grounds for his Claim, and the Duties of Receiving

On the Grounds for the Claim. Know that to no one is the *zakah* due except to a free Moslem belonging to one of the eight groups mentioned in the Book of Allah[81] and being neither a Hashimite[82] nor a Muttalibite,[83] No *zakah* is expended to an unbeliever, or to a slave, or to a Hashimite, or to a Muttalibite. The minor and the insane, however, may enjoy the *zakah* if they have a guardian (*Wali*) to receive it on their behalf.

Let us now discuss each of the eight above mentioned groups.

The first group comprises the paupers (*al-fuqara*).[84] The pauper (*al-faqir*) is he who has no wealth and is unable to earn a living. If the person possesses his daily food and clothing, he will not be a pauper but a poor man (*miskin*).[85] If he possesses half his daily food then he is a pauper. If he possesses a shirt but not a towel, or a shoe, or trousers and the value of the shirt be less than to enable him to secure these articles as it befits paupers, then he is a pauper because he lacks that which he needs and is unable to secure it. That the pauper should not possess anything except an article wherewith to cover his nakedness is inordinate and on the whole no such persons exist. Nor does the person cease to

81. *Surah* IX: 60; see above, p.23.
82. Descendants of Hashim, great-grandfather of the Prophet.
83. Descendants of Al-Muttalib, great-granduncle of the Prophet.
84. Singular *faqir* for which pauper or poverty-stricken has been used throughout this book.
85. This has been rendered poor or a poor man throughout.

be in poverty because he is accustomed to beg. Therefore, begging is not considered a means of earning a living. But if the person is able to earn a living he will no longer be a pauper. If he were able to earn his living by means of an instrument which he does no possess, then he would be a pauper and it would be permissible to purchase the instrument for him. If he were able to earn a living [only] through means unworthy of his honour [202] and not befitting his station, then he would be a pauper. If he were a student of jurisprudence or law and work in order to earn his living would prevent him from continuing his studies then he would be regarded a pauper and his ability to secure a living will not be taken into consideration. If he were a devotee and work to secure a living would prevent him from fulfilling the act of worship and observing the set hours of prayer, let him work for his livelihood as much as possible because his work to earn a living is the more important. The Apostle said, "To seek an honest living is an obligation second only to a religious ordinance [in its importance]."[86] 'Umar said, "To earn a living in a dubious way is better than begging." If he were taken care of by his father or by one under obligation to support him, then he would not be a pauper because this manner of securing livelihood is easier than earning it through work.

The second group comprises the poor (*al-masakin*)[87] A poor man (*miskin*) is he whose income is not sufficient to cover his expenses. Thus, a person may possess a thousand dirhams and yet be poor while another may own nothing more than an ax and a rope and yet be rich. Neither the little house in which the man may be living nor the garment with which he covers his nakedness does remove him from the category of being poor. The same is true of the furniture of his little house. In other words nothing which, in his

86. Unidentified.
87. Sing, miskin, for which poor or a poor man has been used throought this book.

position and station, he needs and possesses would make any difference. [He may possess these things and yet be poor]. Similarly, the books of jurisprudence which he may possess do not make him rich, because he is in need of them. If he should possess nothing but these books he is under no obligation to pay the *zakah* due on breaking the fast of Ramadan. The rule which governs the possession of books is the same as that which governs the possession of garments and home furniture, for a man is in need of all these. neverthelesses, he should understand the real need which the book fulfils. He needs if for three-purposes: for instruction, for deriving benefit for himself, and for recreation through reading. The last is not considered [a valid purpose] and involves the collection of books of poetry and history and the like, none of which are of any use in the hereafter. The collection of such books is of no use in this world except as means of recreation and pleasure. These books are, therefore, sold for [the payment of] expiation and the *zakah* due on breaking the fast of Ramadan, and their possession removes from the person the name of poor.

If he should possess some books for the pleasure of using them in instruction in order to earn his livelihood, in the same way as the tuitor and the teacher do in return for a certain fee, books would then be his tools and, therefore, would not be sold. The rule which governs them is the same as that which governs the tools of tailors and other artisans.

If his purpose in collecting books were to study for the fulfillment of a *fard kifayah* they would not be sold and his possession of them would not rob him of the name poor, because the need for such study is grave.

The collection of books for the purpose of deriving benefits from them and for the sake of learning their contents for himself, such as his collecting medical books in order to [learn how to] administer treatment to himself, or books of sermons in order to read their admonitions and heed their warning, is not necessary at all if a physician or a preacher were living in town. Otherwise, he needs them.

Again he may not need to read a certain book except after the lapse of a certain period of time, in which event the book should be retained as long as its owner needs it. The most reasonable thing to say is that whatever the man does not need within the course of the current year may be spared and dispensed with.

If a person should have something left over from his daily food he would be under obligation to pay the *zakah* due on breaking the fast of Ramadan. Since we reckon food on the basis of a day we should reckon home furniture and bodily clothing on the basis of a year. Consequently, the summer clothes are not sold in winter time not the winter clothes in the summer. And books in this respect, have closer resemblance to clothes and furniture than to anything else.

A person may possess two copies of the same book and, therefore, has need of only one of them. If he should say that the one was more correct while the other was more beautiful and, therefore, he would need both of them, we would say, "You should be content with the more correct copy and sell the more beautiful, and you should let pleasure and luxury alone." If he should have two versions of a work on the same subject, the one extensive and the other brief, and his purpose of having the work should be deriving benefit for himself, let him content himself with the extensive, but if his purpose should be one of instruction and teaching, he would then be in need of both the extensive and brief versions for each possesses distinctive features not found in the other.

Cases like these are numerous and unlimited, and therefore, have not been dealt with in the science of jurisprudence. We have not touched upon the subject under jurisprudence, but mention it here because of the widespread nature of these and similar conditions and to point out that the position here taken is superior to the others. Nevertheless, it is impossible to exhaust the study of all these cases because such an undertaking will require the further investigation into each particular house, its size, the quantity, number, and kind of its furniture, and even the kind of clothing the person possesses. These things have no exact definitions and each jurisprudent applies his own interpretation in an attempt to perfect definitions and thereby avoid the dangers of dubiosities. The pious person chooses the safest course of conduct, abandoning what causes him to doubt what does not cause him to doubt. The ambiguous intermediate positions which fall between the two definite and clear opposite extremes are indeed numerous and nothing saves a person from being entangled in them except [extreme] precaution.

The third group comprises the agents (*al-'ami-lun*).[88] These are the workers who collect the *zakah* except the caliph and the judge. [The list] includes the superintendent (*'arif*), the recorder (*katib*), the collector (*mustawfi*), the keeper (*hafiz*), and the porter (*naqqal*). They are paid alike, and if any money is left from the eighth [of the whole] after all have been paid it is transferred to the [portion of the other] groups, and if [the amount] proves too little it will be supplemented from other revenues.

The fourth group comprises those whose hearts are reconciled [to Islam] (*al-mu'allafah qulubuhum*).[89] These are the nobles who embraced Islam. They are obeyed and respected among their followers, and by giving them [a portion of the *zakah*] they are confirmed in Islam while their peers and followers are attracted and encouraged.

The fifth group comprises those in captivity (*al-mukatabun*).[90] Their portion is paid to their masters although it is permissible to pay it directly to them. The master, however, does not pay any of his *zakah* to the slave who is ransoming himself because the latter is still his slave.

---

88. *Surah* IX: 60.
89. See above, p. 23.
90. Cf. above, p.8.

The sixth group comprises those in debt (*al-gharimun*).[91] A debtor is a pauper who has borrowed [some money for the execution of something] righteous something permissible. If he should borrow the money for an evil purpose he should not be given it unless he should repent. If he were rich, his debt should to be settled [with money from the *zakah* funds] unless he had incurred his debt for the welfare [of the community] or for the settlement of a dispute or an outbreak [of violence].

[203] The seventh group comprises the warriors (*ghuzah*)[92] who are not inscribed in the commissary registry (*diwan al-muriaziqah*). Although they may be wealthy they receive a portion of the *zakah* as a subsidy in time of war.

The eighth group comprises the wayfarers sing. (*ibn-al-sabil*). A wayfarer is one who has set out from his own town on a trip the purpose of which is not evil, or one passing the town for a purpose of the same nature. If such a person were a pauper (*faqir*) he would be given aid [from the *zakah* fund], and if he were possessed of some wealth in another place he would be given aid in accordance to his need.

If you should say, "How then are these qualities known?", we would say: Pauperism (*faqr*) and poverty (*maskanah*) depend upon the word of the recipient, who should not be required to produce any evidence or swear an oath. Rather, he should be taken at his word if he were not an established liar. War and travel are matters of the future. Consequently, anyone who announces his intention of embarking on a war expedition should be taken at his word and given aid from the *zakah* fund. If he should not carry out his announced intention the aid which was given to him should be withdrawn and taken back. As to the other groups evidence should be produced.

These are then the grounds for the claim. As to the

91. *Surah* IX: 60; sing *gharim*.
92. Lit. raiders. Cf. *Surah* IX: 60.

amount which is given to each, a discussion of it is forthcoming.

On the Duties of the Recipient

The duties of the recipient are five. The first duty is that the recipient should know that Allah has ordained the expenditure of [a portion of] *zakah* on him for the purpose of removing his cares and to makes all his worries into one single [concern]. For Allah has imposed upon creation the requirement that their concern in life be focussed upon one thing, namely Allah himself and the last day. This is what is meant by the words of Allah when He said, "And I have not created jinn and men but that they should worship Me."[93] But whereas [divine] wisdom has ordained that man should be subject to desires and needs which divert his attention [from devotion to Allah divine] generousity ordained that he be blessed with bounties suficient to meet those needs. Consequently, Allah made wealth abundant and caused it to flow into the hands of His servants to be for them a means wherewith to meet their needs and free themselves from want in order to devote their time exclusively to His worship and service. To some He gave plentifully and made their wealth a cause of plague and torment, thereby exposing them to the danger [of destruction]. Others He loved and consequently shielded from [the evils of] this world, in the same way as a pitying man guards his patient against injuries. Consequently, He removed from them the luxuries of this world and gave them provisions according to their necessities by placing upon the rich the responsibility of supplying their needs, so that the task of toiling and labouring to earn a living might fall on the rich, while its benefits flow to the paupers [and the poor]. As a result [the paupers and the poor] can devote their lives to the worship of Allah and prepare themselves for what

93. *Surah* LI: 56.

lies beyond death. Neither the luxuries of this world will divert them from the worship of Allah nor poverty and distress from the preparation for the hereafter. Of such is the ideal grace and blessings. Therefore, it befits the poverty-stricken to know the value of poverty and to realize that the bounty of Allah to him is more [manifest] in those things which Allah has withheld from him than in those which He has granted him, as we shall establish and explain in the Book on Poverty. Let him therefore, accept what ever Allah has given him in way of livelihood and regard it as an aid for him in his worship of Allah, and let him, [when enjoying these gifts], have only one single purpose: that through them he may receive thrength to serve Him. If, however, he finds himself unable to do this let him expend those gifts and use them for the attainment of those things which Allah has made permissible.

If he should use [these gifts] as an aid to disobey Allah he would be ungrateful to Allah, denying His blessings and deserving His disfavour and wrath.

The second duty of the recipient is that he should thank the giver, wish him good, and speak well of him. His good wishes, however, should be such as would not remove the giver from being only an instrument [in the hands of Allah], rather it should bring out the fact that the giver is only the means through which the grace of Allah has been extended to him and by which it has reached him. It is true that the means have their own place and importance but this does not and should not prevent the recipient from acknowledging that all blessings come to him from Allah. The Apostle of Allah said, "He who is not grateful to men is not grateful, Allah."[94] Furthermore, Allah Himself praised and commended his servants at several occasions for their good works although He Himself is the creator of those works and the author of man's ability and will to do them. Thus He said,

94. Al-Tirmidhi, al-Barr w-al-Silah: 35.

"How excellent a servant, one who turned to Us was he!"[95] as well as other similar things.

In his good wishes for the giver, let the recipient say, "May Allah purify thy heart together with the hearts of the righteous, and with the good works of the upright and virtuous may He render thy works acceptable and just, and along with the spirits of the martyrs may He bless thine." The Apostle said "Whoever doeth unto you a favour, recompense him, but if ye be not able to do so, wish him good until ye ascertain that ye have recompensed him."[96]

Among the signs of gratitude is to overlook and conceal the defects of the gift whenever it is defective, and to avoid belittling and finding fault with it. Nor should the recipient reproach the giver with stinginess if the latter should withhold [something] from him. On the contrary he should magnify the man's gift both before men and before himself; for it is the duty of the giver the belittle his gift, and the duty of the recipient is to magnify it and show his gratitude. Each man should, therefore, fulfil his duty. There is no discrepancy is this because the belittling of the gift and the magnifying of it counterbalance each other. It is beneficial, therefore, for the giver to observe the methods of belittling his gifts while the opposite process is harmful to him.

All this does not militate against seeing and acknowledging that all blessings come from Allah. He who fails to realize that the means through which he had received the blessing is nothing but an instrument [in the hands of Allah] goes astray; and to regard the instrument as the origin is evil and disapproved.

The third duty of the recipient is that he should examine what he receives and if he should find out that it was not of a lawful source he should abstain therefrom. For he who fears Allah will be given his livelihood by Allah from whence he does not reckon. And he who abstains from what is

---

95. *Surah* XXXVIII: 44.
96. Al-Tayalisi: 1895.

unlawful will not suffer want but will receive his needs from lawful sources [opened to him by Allah]. Let him, therefore, accept nothing from the Turks, the soldiers, the agents of magistrates, and those whose income is mostly unlawful, unless he be in dire distress. Similarly, if he does not definitely know to whom the gift which has been offered to him belongs, [204] he may take of it according to his need and necessity. The legal opinion on this kind [of property] is that it should be given away in alms as will be explained in the Book on the Lawful and the Unlawful. For if the person were unable to avail himself of something lawful and had to take what was within reach, his taking of it would not constitution partaking of the *zakah* because no *zakah* would obtain when the property on which it had been paid is unlawful.

The fourth duty of the recipient is to guard against the pitfalls of doubt and ambiguity regarding the amount of the *zakah* which he may take. He should not take anything except the amount permissible to him to take, and should not touch it unless he were certain that his claim to it was established. If his claim were through a deed of manumission (*kitabah*)[97] or through a debt, he should not take anything in excess of that debt; and if his claim were through his work as a collector he should not accept anything more than his rightful share--if he were offered more. he should decline the offer. For the money does not belong to the giver so that he can dispense with it as he wishes. If the recipient were travelling he should not take anything in excess to the amount sufficient to defray the expenses of his provisions and the cost of hiring the mount to the place of his destination. If he were on a war expedition he should not take anything beyond what he needs of war, especially horses and arms, the amount of which and the expenses thereof

97. Lit. writing. It is a deed of manumission granted to a slave in return for money paid. See *Surah* XXIV: 33; cf. Deut. XV: 12-15. See also above, p.8.

are determined independently and have no limit. The same is true of the provisions of travel. The pious thing for the recipient to do is to ignore what causes him to doubt for what does not cause him to doubt.

If he should receive something on the grounds of poverty, he should first examine the furniture of his house as well as his clothes and books and see whether there are things with which he could dispense or expensive things which he could exchange for cheaper ones and expend the difference. All these things depend primarily on his own choice and opinion and involve two [opposite] states: one which clearly establishes that he is deserving and the other that he is not. Between the two lie several uncertain and questionable states. And he who plays with fire is liable to get burned. In this thing one has to rely upon the word of the recipient and take it as its face value. The needy persons, in estimating their needs, are either very strict or very generous. The pious is apt to be very strict while the unscrupulous is inclined to be generous to an extent where he deems himself in need of many [unnecessary] things, all of which the Law abhors.

When the amount of his need has been definitely ascertained, he should not reach for more but should take an amount sufficient for his need over a period of one year beginning with the time of payment. For this is the limit which the Law allows, since with the lapse of each year the source of the income increases. Furthermore, the Apostle of Allah [was wont] to store up the provisions of one whole year for his family.[98] This is the nearest thing towards a definition of the status of the pauper and the poor. If the recipient would limit himself to the need of one month or even that of one day he would draw closer to piety.

The views and opinions held by the learned men with regard to the amount which a person could receive from the *zakah* and the *sadaqah* are varied and many. Some would

98. Al-Tirmidhi, JIhad: 40.

go to the limit in reducing the amount and require that the person limit himself to no more than his daily food, insisting on following the words of the tradition which Sahl ibn-al-Hanza-liyah[99] related to the effect that the Apostle of Allah had forbidden a person to beg because he was rich. On being asked what made that person rich the Apostle replied, "[His ability to procure] his dinner and supper."[100] Others said that a person may receive as much as he wishes provided he does not go beyond the limit which separates the rich from the poor. This limit is [marked by the possession of] the minimum amount[101] on which the *zakah* is due. Others hold that it is [marked by the possession of] fifty dirhams or the possession of its equivalent in gold, basing their opinion on a tradition reported on the authority of ibn-Mas'ud who related that the Apostle of Allah once said, "He who begs despite the fact that he has riches sufficient for his needs will be brought forth on the day of resurrection with his face full of scars and scratches." On being asked "What manner of riches will suffice his needs?", he replied. "Fifty dirhams or their equivalent in gold."[102] It has been said, however, that the reporter[103] of this tradition was not reliable. Others still say that the possession of forty dirhams or their equivalent in gold marks the distinction between the rich and the poor, and base their contention on a tradition from the *isnad* of which a name has dropped (*munqati'*),

---

99. A.H. 56/A.D. 676; see ibn-Sa'd, vol. VII. pt. 2, p. 124, Ibn-al-Athir, vol. IV. p. 37.
100. Cf. Abu-Dawud, *zakah*: 24.
101. *Nisab.*
102. Al-Nasa'i, *zakah*: 87.
103. The chain of authority (*isnad*) given by Al-Nasa'i is as follows: Ahmad the Sulayman, Yahya ibn-Adam, Sufyan al-Thawri, Hakim ibn-Jubayr, Muhammad ibn-'Abd-al-Rahman ibn-Yazid, his father, 'Abdullah ibn-Mas'ud, the Apostle. The weak link was Hakim ibn-Jubayr. Consequently, al-Nasa'i states that Sufyan had heard the same tradition from Zubayd [ibn-al-Harith] on the same authority. Al-Nasa'i, *zakah*: 87.

related by 'Ata' ibn-Yasar to the effect that the Apostle of Allah once said, "He who begs while he possesses an ounce[104] [of gold] is insolent in his begging."[105]

On the other hand others have gone to the extreme in generosity and said that a person may take as much as would buy him a whole village which will make him independent for the rest of his life, or as much as would establish him in a business that will make him secure for the rest of his days, since this is what they believe a rich person should have. 'Umar said, "When ye give, enrich [those whom ye give]." Consequently, some have gone as far as to say that if a person should lose his wealth and be reduced to poverty, he might take [of the *zakah*] as much as would restore him to his formed state, even though the amount be ten thousand dirhams. But if he should go beyond the limits of moderation [he should be restrained].

When Abu-Ralhah[106] became too much occupied with his garden so as to neglect the observance of the prayer he announced his intention to give it away as a *sadaqah*, but the Apostle said to him, [205] "It is better that you give it to your relatives."[107] Thereupon he settled the garden on Hassan[108] and Abu-Qatadah.[109] A grove of palms, therefore, is sufficient for two and is more than what they need. 'Umar once gave a Bedouin a she-camel and a young camel it was nursing. These instances are related in support of generosity [in the distribution of the *zakah*.

As to the strict [practice of distribution] which will reduce

104. Ar. *uqiyah*, equivalent to forty dirhams.

105. Al-Nasa'i, *zakah*: 89,90.

106. Al-Ansari, Zayd ibn-Sahl, A.H. 34/A.D. 654-655; see Ibn-Sa'd, vol. III, pt. 2, pp. 64-66; Ibn-Qutaybah, p. 138.

107. Al-Bukhari, *zakah*: 45.

108. Ibn-Thabit, the famous poet. He was a cousin of Abu Talhah, and died A.H. 54/A.D. 674. See *Al-Shi'r w-al-Shu'ard'*, pp. 170-73; *Tahdhib al-Asma*, pp. 203-204.

109. Ibn-Rib'i, a distant cousin of Abu-Talhah, died A.H. 54/A.D. 674. See ibn-Sa'd, vol. VI, pp. 8-9.

[the benefits of the *zakah*] to an amount equal] to the daily food [of the individual] or to an ounce of gold, it has been mentioned in connection with the aversion to begging and frequenting the house-door both of which are disapproved and are subject to another rule. In fact to permit the person to receive of the *zakah* as much as would enable him to buy a whole village so that he might become independent for the rest of his life is more probable although it is apt to be extravagant. More moderate is to take an mount sufficient for the current year. To exceed this limit is dangerous and to fall short of it causes distress.

In all these things, unless the Law offers a definite restriction, the independent interpreter of the Law can do nothing but hand down a judgment according to the best of his knowledge and say to the pious [inquirer] what the Apostle himself had said, namely "Consult your own heart although you have been given a dispensation [once, twice or thrice]."[110] But since "sin is heart alluring" the recipient should, whenever he is tempted to take anything [unlawful], fear Allah and not justify his act by a dispensation which he received from learned men [versed] in the letter of the Law [but not in its spirit]. For their dispensations are [subject] to rules and regulations, particular and general, dictated by necessity and expedience and are full of conjectures and dubious [points]. To guard against such dubiousities is characteristic of men of religion and travellers on the path of the hereafter.

The fifth duty of the recipient is to inquire of the owner of the money concerning the amount of his obligation. If the owner should offer him an amount higher than one eighth of the whole *zakah*, he should refuse to accept, for, together with the members of his group, he is entitled only to one eighth of the whole *zakah*. He, therefore, should deduct from the sum which comprises one eighth of the

110. Al-Darimi, Buyu':2.

whole an amount equal to the share of two members of his group.

This inquiry is obligatory on most people, since they usually do not take into consideration this division of the sum [into eight parts and the one eight into at least three portions], either because of ignorance or because of neglect. It is, however, permissible to ignore the inquiry into these things if it does not appear [to the recipient] that there is in them anything which will make them seem probably unlawful. The questions relating to begging and the different degrees of probability will be discussed in the Book on the Lawful and the Unlawful.

SECTION IV

On the Voluntary Almsgiving (sadaqat al-tatawwu'), its Excellence, the Rules of Receiving it and Giving it

On the Excellence of the *Sadaqah*[111]

The excellence of the *sadaqah* is attested by the following traditions. The Apostle said, "Give alms even a single date, for it will satisfy the hunger [of the starving] and does away with sin as the water extinguishes the flames."[112] He also said, "Guard yourselves against Hellfire even by giving half a date, and if ye have none to give, speak a kindly word."[113] And again, "No Moslem will ever give a bushel of dates from wealth lawfully earned, and Allah accepts nothing but the lawful, without its being accepted by Allah, who will tend it in the same way as any one of you tends his young camel or colt, until it grows and multiplies so as to become as great as [Mt.] Uhud."[114] The Apostle also said to Abu-al-Darda', "If you happen to cook some soup be sure to put plenty of water and to invite your neighbours to par-take of it."[115] And again the Apostle said, "Never has a man given alms generously without receiving from Allah the assurance that his heirs will be worthy of the inheritance which he leaves

111. For difference between *sadaqah* and *zakah* see above, p. 3. This section deals with the *sadaqah* proper. It must be remembered, however, that Al-Ghazzali often uses the two terms inter-changeably.
112. Unidentified.
113. Al-Bukhari, *zakah*: 9.
114. Cf. *ibid., zakah*: 8. al-Tirmidhi. *zakah*:2.
115. Muslim, *al-Birr w-al-Silah* 142.

behind."[116] He also said, "Every man will stand under the shadow of his alms until Allah brings all to judgement."[117] And again, "A single *sadaqah* closes seventy gates of evil."[118] And again, "Alms given in secret [206] turn away the wrath of Allah."[119] And on another occasion he said, "The reward of him who gives alms from his abundance is not superior to that of him who receives alms because of need."[120] Perhaps what is meant here is [the recipient] who seeks to satisfy his [physical] needs in order to devote himself exclusively to the duties of religion. Consequently, he will be on a par with the giver who, through his gifts, seeks the welfare of his own religion.

The Apostle was once asked, "Which *sadaqah* is best?" To which he replied," "That which you give when you are in good health and expect many more years of life, despite the fact that your resources are meagre and regardless of your fear of want, not that which you give when you are on your death-bed."[121] On another occasion the Apostle addressed his Companions saying, "Give alms." Thereupon one of them said, "I have one dinar," and the Apostle replied, "Spend it on yourself." The man then said, "I have another dinar," and the Apostle answered, "Spend it on your wife." Again the man said, "I have another," and the Apostle replied, "Spend it on you child." Once again the man said, "I have another," and the Apostle answered, "Spend it on your servant." When for the last time the man said, "I have another dinar," the Apostle replied "You should know best how to dispense with it."[122]

At another time the Apostle said "The *sadaqah* for the family of Muhammad is unlawful because it is made of men's

---

116. Unidentified.
117. Unidentified.
118. Cf. al-Baghdadi, *Ta'rihh Baghdad*, vol. VIII: p.207.
119. Cf. al-Tirmidhi, *zakah* : 28.
120. Unidentified.
121. Al-Bukhari, *zakah* : II; Dawud, Wasaya: 3.
122. Al-Nasa'i, *zakah* :54.

filth."[123] And again, "Remove from the beggar the necessity of begging, even though it be with a morsel of food as small as the head of a bird."[124] He also said, "Had the beggar been truthful, no one who had turned him empty away would prosper."[125] Jesus said, "The angels will not enter the house of him who turneth a beggar empty away."[126] It was the practice of our own Prophet to insist on doing certain things himself and to entrust their performance to no one. These were getting ready his ablution water at night and setting it aside under a cover and handing the alms to the poor with his own hand.[127] The Apostle said, "The poor man is not he who is dismissed with a couple of dates, or a couple of mouthfuls, rather the poor man is he who abstains from begging. Read if you wish [what Allah had said of such men], 'They ask not of men with importunity.' "[128] On another occasion the Apostle said, "Not a single Moslem gives a brother Moslem a garment without, in return for his gift, enjoying the protection of Allah until the last shred of that garment falls off the shoulders of the man to whom it had been given."[129]

In history the excellence of the *sadaqah* is attested by the following:

'Urwah ibn-al-Zubayr[130] once said, "[During her life time] 'A'ishah gave fifty thousand [dinars] in alms, yet her garment was full of patches." Commenting on the words of Allah, "Who for His love bestow their food on the poor, the orphans, and the captives,"[131] Mujahid said, "This means that though longing for it themselves, they give their food to the poor,

---

123. *Ibid., zakah* : 95.
124. Unidentified.
125. Unidentified.
126. Cf. Matt. XXV: 34-45.
127. Unidentified.
128. Cf. *Surah* II: 274; al-Bukhari, *zakah* : 54.
129. Al-Tirmidhi, Qiyamah: 41.
130. A.H. 94/A.D. 712-713; see ibn-Qutaybah, p. 114.
131. *Surah* LXXVI: 8.

the orphans, and the captives." 'Umar [ibn-al-Khattab] was wont to say, "O Allah! Grant plenty and abundance unto the generous among us; haply they may share it with those of us who are in need." 'Abd-al-'Aziz ibn-'Umar[132] used to say, "Prayer brings you half the way to the King, fasting brings you to His door, and almsgiving brings you before His throne." Ibn-abi-al-Ja'd said, "Verily a single *sadaqah* closes away seventy gates of evil." He also regarded secret alms seventy times superior to those given in public, and that each [is capable of] dislocating the jaws of seventy devils. Ibn-Mas'ud said, "Once upon a time there was a man who for seventy years worshipped and obeyed Allah. Then suddenly be committed a grave sin and marred his record. One day he passed by a poor man and gave him a loaf of bread. Thereupon Allah forgave his sin and restored to him the credit of the seventy years of worship and obedience.

Luqman once told his son, "Whenever you commit a sin [atone for it by] giving alms." At another time Yahya ibn-Mu'adh said, "I know of no grain which outweighs the mountains of the whole world except the grain of alms." On another occasion 'Abd-al-'Aziz ibn-Rawwad[133] said, " It used to be said that three things were among the treasures of Paradise. These were: concealing one's illness, giving alms in secret, and maintaining silence under afflictions." This has also been related as an authentic tradition the *isnad* of which goes back to the Apostle.

'Umar ibn-al-Khattab said, "Once upon a time the works of man vied with one another in excellence and the *sadaqah* declared its superiority to all the rest."

It was the custom of 'Abdullah ibn-Umar to give sugar in alms saying, "I have heard Allah say, 'Ye shall never attain

---

132. 'Umar ibn-'Abd-al-Aziz C, 'Abd-al-Aziz 'ibn-Umayr in SM. 'Abd-al-'Aziz ibn-Umar in B. which reading is correct. 'Abd-al-Aziz ibn-'Umar died in A.H. 68/A.D. 764; see al-Tàbari, vol. III, p.40: *skadhardi al-Dhakab*, vol. I, p.219.

133. A.H. 159/A.D. 775-776; see ibn-Sa'd, vol. V, p.362.

righteousness until ye give alms of that which ye love,'[134] and Allah knows that I am fond of sugar."

Al-Nakha'i said once, "If anything be set aside for Allah it should have no defect, for that would displease me."

'Ubayd ibn'Umayr[135] once said, "On the day of resurrection people will be assembled for judgment as hungry as ever, as thirsty as ever, and as naked as ever. Those who, in their lifetime, for love of Allah have given the hungry something wherewith to satisfy their hunger, will be filled; those who have given the thirsty something wherewith to quench their thirst, will be refreshed; and those who have given the naked something wherewith to clothe themselves, will be clothed."

[207] Al-Hasan [Al-Basri] said, "If Allah had so desired He could have made you all rich, not a single poor or pauper among you. But He had willed that some of you be responsible for the support of the others." At another time al-Sha'bi said, "He who does not regard his need to the reward attending his alms greater than that of the recipients of the alms themselves renders his almsgiving useless and, as it were, smites his own face therewith." On another occasion Malik said, "We see no harm in the rich man's drinking of the water which he has donated to be served in the mosque because such water is intended for the use of the thirsty in general and not solely for the benefit of the needy and the poor."

Once upon a time Al-Hasan [Al-Basri] passed by a slave-trader accompanied by a maid for sale. Turning to the trader Al-Hassan said, "Would you accept a dirham or two for the maid?" "No," said the trader. Thereupon al-Hasan replied, "Then go your way. Allah Himself has been content with but a farthing and a single mouthful for a dark-eyed houri."[136]

---

134. *Surah* III: 86.
135. A.H. 68/A.D. 687-688; see ibn-Qutaybah, pp. 221-222.
136. Cf. *Surah* LVI: 22-23.

On Secrecy and Publicity in the Giving of Alms

The paths of the seekers after truth have diverged in pursuing this subject. Some have been disposed to give secrecy the preference while others have been inclined to regard publicity as the more excellent. We shall now discuss the meaning of each, point out the good and the evil therein, and finally bring to light the exact truth of the whole matter.

Secrecy has five advantages. The first is that it better conceals the identity of the recipient. For his receiving alms in public is disgraceful to his manhood. It bares his need and obliges him to relinquish the desirable qualities of self-restraint and temperance, qualities because of which he is regarded rich by the ignorant.

The second [advantage] is that the maintenance of secrecy in the giving of alms is safer for the hearts and the tongues of men who many be otherwise moved to envy and driven to reproach by thinking that the person has received aid without really needing it or that he has taken more than he actually needs. For envy, suspicion, and backbiting are among the major sins, and to guard men against such sins is very important. Ayyub al-Sakhtiyani[137] once said, "Indeed it has always been my practice to avoid putting on a new garment lest I provoke the spirit of jealousy and envy in my neighbours." Another ascetic said, "Many a time I would relinquish one thing and refrain from another simply for the sake of my brethren who might have wondered wherefrom I have gotten them."

It has also been related that Ibrahim al-Taymi was once seen wearing a new shirt and consequently some of his brethren asked him saying, "Wherefrom have you gotten this?" To which he replied, "It was given to me by my brother Khaythamah,[138] but if I had known that his family had any

137. Also al-sikhtiyani; died A.H. 131/A.D. 748-749; see ibn-Sa'd, vol. VII, pt. 2, pp. 14-17; ibn-Qutaybah, pp. 238-239, al-Sam'ani, fol. 292b-293a.

138. Ibn-'Adb-al-Rahman; see ibn-Sa'd, vol. VI, pp. 200-201.

knowledge of it I would have not accepted it."

The third [advantage] of secrecy is that it aids the giver to keep his good works secret, for to give in secret is far superior to giving in public, and to help one do good is itself good. But secrecy is broken whenever the news are made known to more than two individuals, at which time the identity of the giver becomes public property.

A certain man once gave one of the learned men something in public but the latter declined the offer. At another time another person gave him something in secret and he accepted it. Questioned concerning [his behaviour] he said, "This man has acted with politeness and concealed his good deed, consequently I accepted his gift. The other has acted rudely, therefore, I rejected his gift."

A certain Sufi was once given something in the midst of a crowd publicly, but he refused to accept it. Thereupon the giver said to him, "Do you reject that which Allah has given thee?" The Sufi replied saying, "You have associated others besides Allah in that which pertains to Him alone. Therefore, I return to you your sin of association." On another occasion one of the gnostics accepted in secret something which he had rejected in public. Asked [by the giver concerning his action] he replied, "You have publicly disobeyed Allah I refused to be your accomplice in your sin. When, however, you obeyed Him in secret, I helped you in your obedience." At another time Al-Thawri said, "If I were sure that there was among them one who would not talk about or discuss his alms I would have accepted his gifts."

The fourth [advantage of secrecy is that it helps to spare the recipient the humiliation attending the receipt of alms in public]. For to receive alms in public is humiliating and insulting to the recipient, and the believer need not expose himself to humiliation. Thus one of the learned men was wont to accept alms in secret, but refuse them in public saying, "To receive alms in public is degrading to learning and humiliating to its torch bearers. Hence I never accept anything which degrades learning and humilities its torch bearers."

The fifth [advantage] is avoiding [the necessity of] sharing [the alms with those who may be present at the time of giving]. For the Apostle said, "Those who happen to be present when a man receives a gift are his partners therein.[139] That the gift is silver or gold does not change its being a gift. The Apostle said, "The best gift which a man can give his brother is silver or bread." He thus made silver by itself a gift.

In short the practice of giving in the presence of a crowd publicly is viewed with disfavour unless it is done with the consent of all present. Even then the practice is questionable.

Publicity in the giving of alms as well as open discussion of gifts has four advantages. These are as follows:

The first advantage of publicity is that it promotes sincerity, truthfulness, freedom from affectation and hypocrisy.

The second advantage of publicity is that it does away with vainglory and haughtiness, affirming servitude to Allah and poverty instead. It frees man from pride and self-sufficiency, and makes him indifferent to popular acclaim. A certain gnostic once said to one of his disciples, "Do not, under any condition, conceal the fact that you have been the recipient of alms. For when you receive alms and hide not the fact one of two things will ensure: either you lose favour with some people, a thing which is safer for your religion and more wholesome to your soul, or grow in the regards of others because you have revealed the truth. This is exactly what your brother desires because his reward increases [208] as your love to him grows greater and your respect to him becomes more profound. You also would be rewarded if you were instrumental in bringing about the

---

139. Unidentified.

increase in his reward."

The third advantage is that the gnostic is not mindful of anybody other than Allah. His attitude to Him is the same in secret and in public. Consequently, and disagreement or difference between the attitude of the individual towards Allah in secret and his attitude towards Him in public constitutes a sin against the Unity of Allah. Thus one of the gnostics once said, "We were wont to pay no attention to the prayers of him whose practice it was to accept [alms] in secret and reject them in public." To aim at pleasing men, whether they are at the moment present or absent, impairs the state [of mind which man should have towards Allah]. Man should, therefore, be mindful of no one other than the one and only Allah.

The story has been told that a certain teacher was extremely fond of one of his pupils (sing *murid*) but the other pupils resented the [apparent] favouritism. The teacher, desiring to prove to the pupils the superiority of his favourite, give each one of them, including the favourite, a chicken and ordered them to disband into solitary spots where each could kill his chicken without being seen by anyone else. All except the favourite pupil did what the teacher asked them to do. On being asked by the teacher why he failed to carry out his command, the favourite pupil replied, "I could not find a secluded place where no one would see me, because wherever I went Allah saw me." Thereupon the teacher said, "It is for this reason that I favour this pupil, because he is mindful of no one but Allah."

The fourth is that publicity fulfils the obligation of gratitude. Allah said, "Declare the bounty of the Lord."[140] Secrecy, on the other hand, is a denial of that bounty, and Allah has condemned those who conceal His bounties unto them describing them with niggardliness. Thus he said, "[Verily, Allah loveth not the proud, the vain boaster] who

140. *Surah* XCIII: 11.

are niggardly themselves, and bid others to be niggards, and hide away what Allah hath of his bounty given them."[141] The Apostle said, "Whenever Allah bestows a bounty upon one of His servants, He likes the bounty to be seen."[142]

A certain person once gave something to one of the virtuous, who immediately displayed the gift saying, "This is something from this world wherein publicity is best, but in matters pertaining to the hereafter secrecy is best." For this reason a certain person said, "If you are given something in the presence of a crowd accept it, later returning it in private."

Gratitude and thankfulness for alms is highly recommended. The Apostle said, "He who is not grateful to men is not grateful to Allah."[143] Gratitude takes the place of reward to such an extent that the Apostle once said, "Whoever doeth unto you a favour recompense him, but if ye be no able to do so, wish him good until ye ascertain that ye have recompensed him."[144]

When on one day the emigrants were discussing with the Apostle the question of gratitude and thanks they said, "O Apostle of Allah, never have we seen anybody in whose house we lived as guests and whose property we shared, without fearing that he would run away with all the reward." Thereupon the Apostle replied, "[Fear not], for your thanks and praise are as good as compensation."[145]

Now that you have seen these various advantages know that the differences which exist in them are in reality not basic differences in the problem itself but rather differences in the attitudes [of men] towards the problem. The gist of the matter is that we do not rule that privacy is, under all conditions, the best practice or the publicity is the best.

---

141. *Surah* IV:41.
142. Unidentified.
143. Al-Tirmidhi, al-Birr w-al-Silah: 35.
144. Al-Tayalisi: 1895.
145. Cf. al-Tirmidhi, Qiyamah: 44: Abu-Dawud, Adab:11.

Rather they differ as the intentions differ, and the intentions in turn differ as the attitudes and the individuals differ. Consequently, the sincere person should watch himself carefully lest he be misled by vanity and beguiled by the deception of nature and the artifice of the devil. Artifice and deception and more prevalent in privacy than in publicity, although they affect both.

Deception enters into privacy through the predilection of [human] nature to it, especially because it helps to maintain one's prestige and position before men, shields him against their disfavour and contempt, and spares him the necessity of acknowledging the giver as benefactor and philanthropist. It is a virulent disease which afflicts the soul and through which the devil brings the advantages of privacy home to the individual, thereby persuading him to justify his behaviour with [one of] the five points which we have mentioned [in favour of privacy.].

The criterion of this as well as its acid test in one single thing, namely that the suffering which the individual undergoes, because the fact of his receiving alms has been made public, be just as acute as the suffering which he experiences when one of his adversaries or opponents has received alms and the news of his receiving them has been made known. For if he were interested in shielding people against calumny, envy, and suspicion or desirous to avoid betraying a confidence and anxious to aid a giver conceal his gifts, as well as to safeguard learning against [disgrace and the learned men against] insult, he should know that all these things would result from making public his brother's receipt of alms [just as they would result from making public his own]. If the exposure of his own is harder on him than that of others, then his apprehensions regarding these considerations are untrue and false, resulting from the artifice and the deception of the devil.

Furthermore, to disgrace and discredit learning is forbidden not because it is the learning of this or the other person but simply because it is learning itself. Calumny is forbidden because it is the defamation of a person's honour as such, not because it is the vilification of a particular person's honour.

Anyone observing this point may prove too strong for the devil to subdue, otherwise he will be a man of much activity but little success.

On the other hand human nature may incline to publicity, because through it the individual humours the giver and pleases him thereby encouraging him to do the same again. Moreover, by making the receipt of alms known to the public, the recipient reveals himself extremely grateful so that people might become disposed to honour him and ready to inquire about him and help him.

This is a virulent disease which afflicts the heart. [209] The devil, however, cannot prevail over the religious except by presenting such corruption to him as a part of the Law, telling him that open gratitude is a part of the Law, while concealing it is hypocritical, and reciting to him all the various advantages which we have already mentioned in connection with publicity in order to induce him to make public his thanks. Man's inner purpose and motive, however, is that which we have already described, namely to make people better disposed to help him and be gracious unto him.

The criterion of this as well as its acid test is that the individual should compare his readiness to be thankful in cases where his thanks are neither revealed to the giver nor to the person who intends to extend to him his aid with his readiness to be thankful in the presence of persons who dislike making their gifts known but desire to keep them secret and whose custom is not to give except to one who keeps the news of their gifts secret and refrains from giving thanks. If both these conditions appear equal to him his motive would then truly be the observance of the Law by gratitude and articulate thankfulness. Otherwise, he is deluded. Again if he were moved to gratitude and thanks by the demands of the Law, he should not neglect to fulfil his duty to the giver. If the latter were fond of being thanked publicly the recipient should hide his gratitude and not express his thanks, because it is his duty not to aid the giver to sin, since his expectation of thanks is sinful. But if he should find out that the giver is not fond of being thanked and does not expect or seek it, the recipient should then thank him openly and make his gift known to the public. For this reason the Apostle of Allah said of the person who was praised in his presence, "You have overdone his praise; verily if he were to hear it he would fail," [146] although the Apostle was wont to praise people to their face. This is because he had confidence in their faith and because he was sure that his praise would not harm them but rather would increase their desire and encourage them to do good. On another occasion the Apostle said [pointing] to a certain visitor, "Behold this man is the master of all Bedouins (*ahl al-wabar*).[147] Referring to another he said, "When a celebrity visits you honour him."[148] At another time he heard someone talk and, being pleased with his speech, said, "Verily, there is magic in eloquent speech."[149] He also said, "If any of you should see something worthy in his brother, he should tell him of it for that would make him more desirous to do good."[150] And again, "Whenever the believer is praised, belief grows stronger in his heart."[151]

---

146. Cf. al-Bukhari, Adab: 54.
147. *Ahl al-wabar* is literally the inhabitants of hair tents, i.e. The nomads or the Bedouins. The reference is to Qayas ibn-'Asim who appeared before the Apostle and embraced Islam. Qayas died A.H. 47/A.D. 667-668; see ibn-Sa'd, vol. VII, pt. I, pp. 23-4; ibn-Qutayabah, pp. 153-154; *al-Aghani*, vol. XII, pp. 149-158; abu-al-Fida', vol. I, pp. 196-197.
148. Ibn Majah, Adab: 19.
149. Al-Bukhari, Nikah: 48.
150. Unidentified.
151. Unidentified.

Al-Thawri once said, "He who knows himself will not be harmed by the praise of men." On another occasion he said to Yusuf ibn-Asbat, "Whenever I do you a favour I am more pleased with it than you are because I regard it as one of the blessings of Allah upon me. Consequently, I give thanks to Allah. Unless I see my favour in this light my gratitude will be false."

These details should be observed by anyone who watches his heart, for without these details the works of the senses are the laughing-stock of the devil and the object of his ridicule and malice especially for what seems to be much activity but little profit. It is such knowledge which is described by the following saying, namely, 'Learning one point of such knowledge is better than a year of worship." For through this knowledge worship becomes a living and a vital thing and without it, it dwindles and comes to nought. In short, to take in public and to reject in private is the best and safest policy to follow, Furthermore, no one, in rejecting a gift, should be excessive in his protestations of unworthiness. Rather his knowledge should be complete so that both privacy and publicity would be the same to him. Such a state is like red sulphur, often heard of but never seen.

On which is Better, to Accept Aid from the Sadaqah or from the Zakah[152]

Both Ibrahim al-Khawwas and al-Junayd, as well as many others, held that accepting aid from the *sadaqah* fund was better than accepting it from the *zakah* money, because in sharing the latter the individual competes with the poor and diminishes their means, Furthermore, he may not be able to establish his claim to the benefit from the *zakah* money

152. As has been sown before the term *zakah* represents the legal alms and *sadaqah*, the voluntary. Al-Ghazzali has so far used the two terms interchangeably; now however he uses the *sadaqah* for the voluntary alms and the *zakah* for the legal and obligatory.

or prove himself actually deserving in accordance with the qualifications set down in the Glorious Book. But the *sadaqah* is more general.

Others have said that a person should accept aid from the *zakah* fund rather than from the *sadaqah* money, because in so doing he would be fulfilling the Law.[153] Thus, if all the poor should refrain from accepting aid from the *zakah* fund they would sin. A person should accept [his portion of] the *zakah* [not only] because it places him under no obligation but also because it has been ordained by Allah as a means of livelihood for those needy among His servants. It is, therefore, because of need and necessity that a person accepts *zakah* [money], and he certainly knows his needs.

To accept aid from the *sadaqh* funds is an offence against religion, because ordinarily the benefactor gives only to those of whom he thinks well; while the company of the poor is more conducive to humility and meekness and farther removed from pride; since offtimes a person may accept a *sadaqah* as though it were merely a present and nothing distinct [210] from a present.

These indicate an insistence on the humility and the need of the receiver of the *zakah*. The truth of the matter is that these things vary with each individual depending on the particular state in which he may be at that time and on the kind of intention which he may at that moment entertain. If he were in doubt as to whether or not he was deserving he should not accept anything from the *zakah*. But if he were certain that he was deserving, as, for example, when he has to pay a debt which he had incurred for a just cause and is unable to pay it without aid, then he is certainly entitled to that aid and justified in accepting it.

If a deserving individual were given the choice between accepting aid from the *zakah* or the *sadaqah* and had found out that the person who is to give the *sadaqah* would not

153. Cf. *Surah* IX: 60.

give that particular sum unless he were to accept it, let him by all means choose the *sadaqah,* as the *zakah* which is compulsory would always be paid to its deserving beneficiaries. This would increase charity and better the conditions of the poor.

If the money were to be definitely given as a *sadaqah* any way and on the other hand the acceptance of the *zakah* would not result in distress for the poor, the person would be free to make his choice. In short the arguments in favour of the one or the other vary. On the whole the acceptance of aid from the *zakah* is more conducive to modesty and humility.

LIST OF REFERENCES

Athir, ibn-al, *al-Kamil fi 'l-Ta'rikh,* ed. C.J. Tornberg (Leyden 1867-1874).

Baghdadi, al-, *Ta'rikh Baghdad* (Cairo 1349).

Bukhari, al-, *Sahih* (Bulaq 1296).

Darimi, al-, *Sunan* (Damascus 1349).

Dawud, abu-, *Sunan* (Cario 1280).

Fida', abu-al, *Mukhtasar Ta'rikh al-Bashar* (Constantinople 1286).

Hisham, ibn-, *Sirat Rasul Allah,* ed. F. Wustenfeld (Gottingen 1858-1860).

'Imad al-Hanbali, ibn-al-, *Shadharat al-Dhahab fi Akhtar man Dhahab* (Cairo 1350).

Isfahani, al-, *al-Aghani* (Bulaq 1285).

Manawi, al-, *Fayd al-Qadir, Sharh al-Jami' al-Saghir* (Cairo 1938).

Muslim, *Sahih* (Delhi 1319).

Nasa'i, al-, *al-Mujtaba* (Delhi 1315).

Qutaybah, ibn-, *Kitab al-Ma'arif,* ed. F. Wustenfeld (Gottingen 1850).

Rif'at, Ibrahim, *Mir'at al-Haramayan* (Cairo 1925).

Sa'd, ibn-, *Kitab al-Tabaqat al-Kubra,* ed. E. Sachau and others (Leyden 1905-1921).

Tabari, al-, *Ta'rikh al-Rusul w-al-Muluk,* ed. M.J. de Goeje (Leyden 1879 ff.).

Taylaisi, al-, *Musnad* (Hyderabad 1321).

Tirmidhi, al-, *Sunan* (Cairo 1290).

INDEX OF ARABIC TERMS

INDEX OF PROPER NAMES